W9-AVL-055

iSearch:
English

H. Eric Branscomb
Salem State College

Linda R. Barr
University of the Virgin Islands

Longman

Boston | New York | San Francisco
Mexico City | Montreal | Toronto | London | |Madrid | Munich | Paris
Hong Kong | Singapore | Tokyo | Cape Town | Sydney

Senior Supplements Editor: Donna Campion
Electronic Page Makeup: Big Color Systems, Inc.

iSearch: English, by H. Eric Branscomb and Linda R. Barr

Please visit our Web site at: http://www.ablongman.com

ISBN: 0-321-12411-1

1 2 3 4 5 6 7 8 9 10 - VG - 05 04 03 02

Contents

iSearch: English

Introduction

Your professor assigns a ten-page research paper that's due in two weeks—and you need to make sure you have up-to-date, credible information. Where do you begin? Today, the easiest answer is the Internet—because it can be so convenient and there is so much information out there. But therein lies part of the problem. How do you know if the information is reliable and from a trustworthy source?

iSearch: English is designed to help you select and evaluate research from the Web to help you find the best and most credible information you can. Throughout this guide, you'll find:

- **A practical and to-the-point discussion of search engines.** Find out which search engines are likely to get you the information you want and how to phrase your searches for the most effective results.
- **Detailed information on evaluating online sources.** Locate credible information on the Web and get tips for thinking critically about Web sites.
- **Citation guidelines for Web resources.** Learn the proper citation guidelines for Web sites, e-mail messages, listservs, and more.
- **Web activities for English.** Explore the various ways you can use the Web in your courses through these online exercises.
- **Web links for English.** Begin your Web research with the discipline-specific sources listed in this section. Also included is information about Web resources offered by Allyn & Bacon—these sites are designed to give you an extra boost in your communication courses.

So before running straight to your browser, take the time to read through this copy of *iSearch: English* and use it as a reference for all of your Web research needs.

Conducting Online Research

Finding Sources:
Search Engines and Subject Directories

Your professor has just given you an assignment to give a five minute speech on the topic "gun control." After a (hopefully brief) panic attack, you begin to think of what type of information you need before you can write the speech. To provide an interesting introduction, you decide to involve your class by taking a straw poll of their views for and against gun control, and to follow this up by giving some statistics on how many Americans favor (and oppose) gun control legislation and then by outlining the arguments on both sides of the issue. If you already know the correct URL for an authoritative Web site like Gallup Opinion Polls (<www.gallup.com>) or other sites you are in great shape! However, what do you do when you don't have a clue as to which Web site would have information on your topic? In these cases, many, many people routinely (and mistakenly) go to Yahoo! and type in a single term (e.g., guns). This approach is sure to bring first a smile to your face when the results offer you 200,874 hits on your topic, but just as quickly make you grind your teeth in frustration when you start scrolling down the hit list and find sites that range from gun dealerships, to reviews of the video "Young Guns," to aging fan sites for "Guns and Roses."

Finding information on a specific topic on the Web is a challenge. The more intricate your research need, the more difficult it is to find the one or two Web sites among the billions that feature the information you want. This section is designed to help you to avoid frustration and to focus in on the right site for your research by using search engines, subject directories, and meta-sites.

Search Engines

Search engines (sometimes called search services) are becoming more numerous on the Web. Originally, they were designed to help users search the Web by topic. More recently, search engines have added features which enhance their usefulness, such as searching a particular part of the Web (e.g., only sites of educational institutions—dot.edu), retrieving just one site which the search engine touts as most relevant (like Ask Jeeves <www.aj.com>), or retrieving up to 10 sites which the search engine rank as most relevant (like Google <www.google.com>).

Search Engine Defined

According to Cohen (1999):

> A search engine service provides a searchable database of Internet files collected by a computer program called a wanderer, crawler, robot, worm, or spider. Indexing is created from the collected files, and the results are presented in a schematic order. There are no selection criteria for the collection of files.
>
> A search service therefore consists of three components: (1) a spider, a program that traverses the Web from link to link, identifying and reading pages; (2) an index, a database containing a copy of each Web page gathered by the spider; and (3) a search engine mechanism, software that enables users to query the index and then returns results in a schematic order. (31)

One problem students often have in their use of search engines is that they are deceptively easy to use. Like our example "guns," no matter what is typed into the handy box at the top, links to numerous Web sites appear instantaneously, lulling students into a false sense of security. Since so much was retrieved, surely SOME of it must be useful. WRONG! Many Web sites retrieved will be very light on substantive content, which is not what you need for most academic endeavors. Finding just the right Web site has been likened to finding diamonds in the desert.

As you can see by the definition above, one reason for this is that most search engines use indexes developed by machines. Therefore they are indexing terms not concepts. The search engine cannot tell the difference between the keyword "crack" to mean a split in the sidewalk and "crack"

TYPES OF SEARCH ENGINES

TYPE	DESCRIPTION	EXAMPLES
1st Generation	• Non-evaluative, do not evaluate results in terms of content or authority. • Return results ranked by relevancy alone (number of times the term(s) entered appear, usually on the first paragraph or page of the site)	AltaVista (www.altavista.com/) Excite (www.excite.com) HotBot (www.HotBot.com) InfoseekGo (infoseek.go.com) Ixquick Metasearch (ixquick.com) Lycos (www.lycos.com)
2nd Generation	• More creative in displaying results. • Results are ordered by characteristics such as: concept, document type, Web site, popularity, etc. rather than relevancy.	Ask Jeeves (www.aj.com/) Direct Hit (www.teoma.com/) Google! (www.google.com/) HotLins (www.hotlinks.com/) Simplifind (www.simpli.com/servlet/ SearchMainServlet) SurfWax (www.surfwax.com/) Also see Meta-Search engines below. EVALUATIVE SEARCH ENGINES About.Com (www.about.com) Webcrawler (www.webcrawler.com)
Commercial Portals	• Provide additional features such as: customized news, stock quotations, weather reports, shopping, etc. • They want to be used as a "one stop" Web guide. • They profit from prominent advertisements and fees charged to featured sites.	GONetwork (www.go.com/) Google Web Directory (directory.google.com/) LookSmart (www.looksmart.com/) Open Directory Project (dmoz.org/) NBCi (www.nbci.com) Yahoo! (www.yahoo.com/)
Meta-Search Engines	Run searches on multiple search engines.	There are different types of meta search engines. See the next 2 boxes

Meta-Search Engines
Integrated Result
	• Display results for search engines in one list.
	• Duplicates are removed.
	• Only portions of results from each engine are returned.
		Beaucoup.com (www.beaucoup.com
		Cyber411(www.cyber411. com/)
		Mamma (www.mamma.com/)
		MetaCrawler (www.
		   metacrawler.com/)
		Northern Light
		   (www.northernlight.com/)
		Search (www.search.com)

iSearch: English

(continued)

TYPES OF SEARCH ENGINES, *continued*		
TYPE	DESCRIPTION	EXAMPLES
Meta-Search Engines *Non-Integrated* *Results*	• Comprehensive search. • Displays results from each search engine in separate results sets. • Duplicates remain. • You must sift through all the sites.	Dogpile (www.dogpile.com) Global Federated Search (jin.dis.vt.edu/fedsearch/) GoHip (www.gohip.com) 1Blink (www.1blink.com) ProFusion (www. profusion.com/)

referring to crack cocaine. To use search engines properly takes some skill, and this chapter will provide tips to help you use search engines more effectively. First, however, let's look at the different types of search engines with examples:

QUICK TIPS FOR MORE EFFECTIVE USE OF SEARCH ENGINES

1. Use a search engine:
   - When you have a narrow idea to search;
   - When you want to search the full text of countless Web pages;
   - When you want to retrieve a large number of sites;
   - When the features of the search engine (like searching particular parts of the Web) help with your search.

2. Always use Boolean Operators to combine terms. Searching on a single term is a sure way to retrieve a very large number of Web pages, few, if any, of which are on target.
   - Always check search engine's HELP feature to see what symbols are used for the operators as these vary (e.g., some engines use the & or + symbol for AND).
   - Boolean Operators include:
     AND to narrow search and to make sure that **both** terms are included
        e.g., children AND violence
     OR to broaden search and to make sure that **either** term is included
        e.g., child OR children OR juveniles
     NOT to **exclude** one term
        e.g., eclipse NOT lunar

3. Use appropriate symbols to indicate important terms and to indicate phrases (Best Bet for Constructing a Search According to Cohen (1999): Use a plus sign (+) in front of terms you want to retrieve: +solar +eclipse. Place a phrase in double quotation marks: "solar eclipse" Put together: "+solar eclipse" "+South America").

iSearch: English

4. Use word stemming (a.k.a. truncation) to find all variations of a word (check search engine HELP for symbols).
   - If you want to retrieve child, child's, or children use child* (some engines use other symbols such as !, #, or $)
   - Some engines automatically search singular and plural terms, check HELP to see if yours does.

5. Since search engines only search a portion of the Web, use several search engines or a meta-search engine to extend your reach.

6. Remember search engines are generally mindless drones that do not evaluate. Do not rely on them to find the best Web sites on your topic, use *subject directories* or meta-sites to enhance value (see below).

Finding Those Diamonds in the Desert: Using Subject Directories and Meta-Sites

Although some search engines, like Webcrawler <www.webcrawler.com> do evaluate the Web sites they index, most search engines do not make any judgment on the worth of the content. They just return a long—sometimes very long—list of sites that contained your keyword. However,

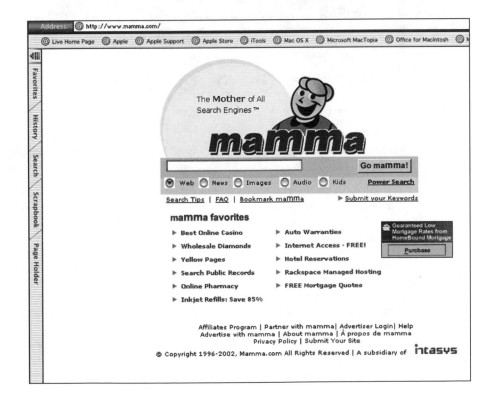

subject directories exist that are developed by human indexers, usually librarians or subject experts, and are defined by Cohen (1999) as follows:

> A subject directory is a service that offers a collection of links to Internet resources submitted by site creators or evaluators and organized into subject categories. Directory services use selection criteria for choosing links to include, though the selectivity varies among services. (27)

World Wide Web subject directories are useful when you want to see sites on your topic that have been reviewed, evaluated, and selected for their authority, accuracy, and value. They can be real time savers for students, since subject directories weed out the commercial, lightweight, or biased Web sites.

Meta-sites are similar to subject directories, but are more specific in nature, usually dealing with one scholarly field or discipline. Some examples of subject directories and Meta-sites are found in the following table.

SMART SEARCHING—SUBJECT DIRECTORIES AND META-SITES	
TYPES—SUBJECT DIRECTORIES	EXAMPLES
General, covers many topics	• Access to Internet and Subject Resources (www2.lib.udel.edu/subj/) • AlphaSearch-Gateway to the "Academic" Web (www.calvin.edu/library/as/) • Argus Clearinghouse (www.clearinghouse.net) • Best Information on the Net (BIOTN) (library.sau.edu:80/bestinfo/) • Federal Web Locator (www.infoctr.edu/fwl/) • Galaxy (galaxy.einet.net) • InfoFinder (home.revealed.net/albee/) • INFOMINE: Scholarly Internet Resource Collections (infomine.ucr.edu/) • InfoSurf: Resources by Subject (www.library.ucsb.edu/subj/) • Librarian's Index to the Internet (www.lii.org/) • Martindale's "The Reference Desk" (www-sci.lib.uci.edu/~martindale/Ref.html) • PINAKES: A Subject Launchpad (www.hw.ac.uk/libWWW/irn/pinakes/pinakes.html) • Refdesk.com (www.refdesk.com/) • Search Engines and Subject Directories (College of New Jersey) (www.tcnj.edu/~library/research/internet_search.html) • Scout Report Signpost (www.signpost.org/signpost/) • Selected Reference Sites (www.mnsfld.edu/depts/lib/mu~ref.html) • WWW Virtual Library (celtic.stanford.edu/vlib/Overview.html)
Subject Oriented	
Communication Studies	• University of Iowa Department of Communication Studies (www.uiowa.edu/~commstud/resources/index-html)
Cultural Studies	• Sara Zupko's Cultural Studies Center (www.popcultures.com)
Education	• Educational Virtual Library (www.csu.edu.au/education/library.html) • ERIC [Education ResourcesInformation Center] (ericir.sunsite.syr.edu/) • Kathy Schrock's Guide for Educators (kathyschrock.net/abceval/index.htm)

(continued)

iSearch: English

SMART SEARCHING—SUBJECT DIRECTORIES AND META-SITES, continued	
TYPES—SUBJECT DIRECTORIES	EXAMPLES
Journalism	• Journalism Resources (bailiwick.lib.uiowa.edu/journalism/) • Journalism and Media Criticism page (www.chss.montclair.edu/english/furr/media.html)
Literature	• Norton Web Source to American Literature (www.wwnorton.com/naal) • Project Gutenberg [Over 3,000 full text titles] (www.gutenberg.net)
Medicine & Health	• PubMed [National Library of Medicine's index to Medical journals, 1966 to present] (www.ncbi.nlm.nih.gov/PubMed/) • RxList: The Internet Drug Index (rxlist.com) • Go Ask Alice (www.goaskalice.columbia.edu) [Health and sexuality
Technology	• CNET.com (www.cnet.com)

Choose subject directories to ensure that you are searching the highest quality Web pages. As an added bonus, subject directories periodically check Web links to make sure that there are fewer dead ends and out-dated links.

Another closely related group of sites are the *Virtual Library* sites, also referred to as Digital Library sites. Hopefully, your campus library has an outstanding Web site for both on-campus and off-campus access to resources. If not, there are several virtual library sites that you can use, although you should realize that some of the resources would be subscription based, and not accessible unless you are a student of that particular university or college. These are useful because, like the subject directories and meta-sites, experts have organized Web sites by topic and selected only those of highest quality.

You now know how to search for information and use search engines more effectively. In the next section, you will learn more tips for evaluating the information that you found.

BIBLIOGRAPHY FOR FURTHER READING

Books

Basch, Reva. *Secrets of the Super Net Searchers*. Wilton, CT: Pemberton, 1996.

Berkman, Robert I. *Find It Fast: How to Uncover Expert Information on Any Subject Online or in Print*. NY: HarperResource, 2000.

VIRTUAL LIBRARY SITES

Public Libraries
- Internet Public Library
- Library of Congress
- New York Public Library

www.ipl.org
lcweb.loc.gov/homepage/lchp.html
www.nypl.org

University/College Libraries
- Bucknell
- Case Western
- Dartmouth
- Duke
- Franklin & Marshall
- Harvard
- Penn State
- Princeton
- Stanford
- ULCA
- William Paterson University

jade.bucknell.edu/
www.cwru.edu/uclibraries.html
www.dartmouth.edu/~library
www.lib.duke.edu/
www.library.fandm.edu
www.harvard.edu/museums/
www.libraries.psu.edu
infoshare1.princeton.edu
www-sul.stanford.edu
www.library.ucla.edu
www.wpunj.edu/library

Other
- Perseus Project [subject specific—classics, supported by grants from corporations and educational institutions]

www.perseus.tufts.edu

iSearch: English

Glossbrenner, Alfred and Emily Glossbrenner. *Search Engines for the World Wide Web*. 2nd ed. Berkeley, CA: Peachpit, 1999.

Hock, Randolph, and Paula Berinstein. *The Extreme Searcher's Guide to Web Search Engines: A Handbook for the Serious Searcher*. Medford, NJ: CyberAge Books, 1999.

Miller, Michael. *Complete Idiot's Guide to Yahoo!* (2000). Indianapolis, IN: Que.

Miller, Michael. *Complete Idiot's Guide to Online Search Secrets*. (2000). Indianapolis, IN: Que.

Paul, Nora, Margot Williams, and Paula Hane. *Great Scouts! CyberGuides for Subject Searching on the Web*. Medford, NJ: CyberAge Books, 1999.

Radford, Marie, Susan Barnes, and Linda Barr. *Web Research: Selecting, Evaluating, and Citing* Boston. Allyn and Bacon, 2001.

Journal Articles

Cohen, Laura B. "The Web as a Research Tool: Teaching Strategies for Instructors." *CHOICE Supplement* 3 (1999): 20–44.

——— "Searching the Web: The Human Element Emerges." *CHOICE Supplement* 37 (2000) 17–31.

Introna, Lucas D., and Helen Nissenbaum. "Shaping the Web: Why the Politics of Search Engines Matters." *The Information Society*, No. 3 (2000): 169–185.

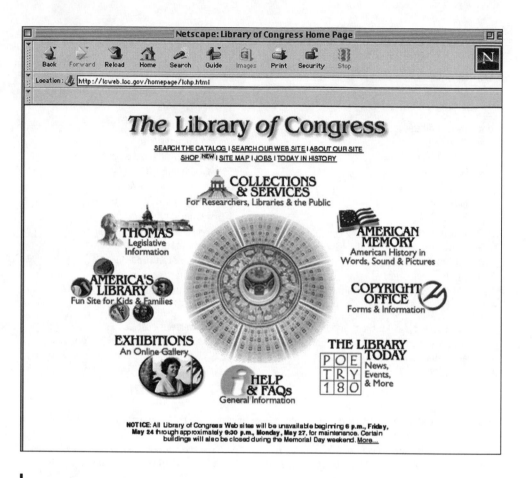

Evaluating Sources on the Web

Congratulations! You've found a great Web site. Now what? The Web site you found seems like the perfect Web site for your research. But, are you sure? Why is it perfect? What criteria are you using to determine whether this Web site suits your purpose?

Think about it. Where else on earth can anyone "publish" information regardless of the *accuracy, currency,* or *reliability* of the information? The Internet has opened up a world of opportunity for posting and distributing information and ideas to virtually everyone, even those who might post misinformation for fun, or those with ulterior motives for promoting their point of view. Armed with the information provided in this guide, you can dig through the vast amount of useless information and misinformation on the World Wide Web to uncover the valuable information. Because practically anyone can post and distribute their ideas on the Web, you need to develop a new set of *critical thinking skills* that focus on the evaluation of

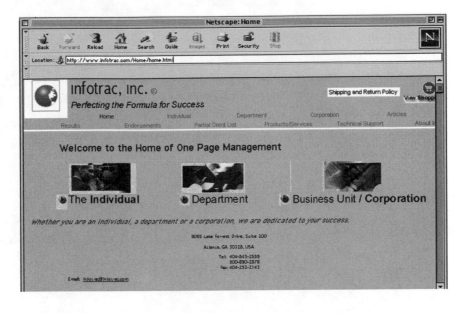

the quality of information, rather than be influenced and manipulated by slick graphics and flashy moving java script.

Before the existence of online sources, the validity and accuracy of a source was more easily determined. For example, in order for a book to get to the publishing stage, it must go through many critiques, validation of facts, reviews, editorial changes, and the like. Ownership of the information in the book is clear because the author's name is attached to it. The publisher's reputation is on the line too. If the book turns out to have incorrect information, reputations and money can be lost. In addition, books available in a university library are further reviewed by professional librarians and selected for library purchase because of their accuracy and value to students. Journal articles downloaded or printed from online subscription services, such as Infotrac, ProQuest, EbscoHost, or other fulltext databases, are put through the same scrutiny as the paper versions of the journals.

On the World Wide Web, however, Internet service providers (ISPs) simply give Web site authors a place to store information. The Web site author can post information that may not be validated or tested for accuracy. One mistake students typically make is to assume that all information on the Web is of equal value. Also, in the rush to get assignments in on time, students may not take the extra time to make sure that the information they are citing is accurate. It is easy just to cut and paste without really thinking about the content in a critical way However, to make sure you are gathering accurate information and to get the best grade on your assignments, it is vital that you develop your critical ability to sift through the dirt to find the diamonds.

Evaluating Web Sites Using
Five Criteria to Judge Web Site Content:

Accuracy—How reliable is the information?

Authority—Who is the author and what are his or her credentials?

Objectivity—Does the Web site present a balanced or biased point of view?

Coverage—Is the information comprehensive enough for your needs?

Currency—Is the Web site up to date?

Using additional criteria to judge Web site content, including

- **publisher, documentation, relevance, scope, audience, appropriateness of format, and navigation**
- Judging whether the site is made up of **primary (original) or secondary (interpretive) sources**
- Determining whether the information is **relevant** to your research

Web Evaluation Criteria

So, here you are, at this potentially great site. Let's go though some ways you can determine if this site is one you can cite with confidence in your research. Keep in mind, ease of use of a Web site is an issue, but more important is learning how to determine the validity of data, facts, and statements for your use. The five traditional ways to verify a paper source can also be applied to your Web source: *accuracy, authority, objectivity, coverage,* and *currency.*

Content Evaluation

Accuracy   Internet searches are not the same as searches of library databases because much of the information on the Web has not been edited, whereas information in databases has. It is your responsibility to make sure that the information you use in a school project is accurate. When you examine the content on a Web site or Web page, you can ask yourself a number of questions to determine whether the information is accurate.

1. Is the information reliable?
2. Do the facts from your other research contradict the facts you find on this Web page?
3. Do any misspellings and/or grammar mistakes indicate a hastily put together Web site that has not been checked for accuracy?

4. Is the content on the page verifiable through some other source? Can you find similar facts elsewhere (journals, books, or other online sources) to support the facts you see on this Web page?

5. Do you find links to other Web sites on a similar topic? If so, check those links to ascertain whether they back up the information you see on the Web page you are interested in using.

6. Is a bibliography of additional sources for research provided? Lack of a bibliography doesn't mean the page isn't accurate, but having one allows you further investigation points to check the information.

7. Does the site of a research document or study explain how the data was collected and the type of research method used to interpret the data?

If you've found a site with information that seems too good to be true, it may be. You need to verify information that you read on the Web by crosschecking against other sources.

Authority   An important question to ask when you are evaluating a Web site is, "Who is the author of the information?" Do you know whether the author is a recognized authority in his or her field? Biographical information, references to publications, degrees, qualifications, and organizational affiliations can help to indicate an author's authority. For example, if you are researching the topic of laser surgery citing a medical doctor would be better than citing a college student who has had laser surgery.

The organization sponsoring the site can also provide clues about whether the information is fact or opinion. Examine how the information was gathered and the research method used to prepare the study or report. Other questions to ask include:

1. Who is responsible for the content of the page? Although a Webmaster's name is often listed, this person is not necessarily responsible for the content.

2. Is the author recognized in the subject area? Does this person cite any other publications he or she has authored?

3. Does the author list his or her background or credentials (e.g., Ph.D. degree, title such as professor, or other honorary or social distinction)?

4. Is there a way to contact the author? Does the author provide a phone number or e-mail address?

5. If the page is mounted by an organization, is it a known, reputable one?

6. How long has the organization been in existence?

7. Does the URL for the Web page end in the extension .edu or .org? Such extensions indicate authority compared to dotcoms (.com), which are commercial enterprises. (For example, www.cancer.com takes you to an online drugstore that has a cancer information page; www.cancer.org is the American Cancer Society Web site.)

iSearch: English

A good idea is to ask yourself whether the author or organization presenting the information on the Web is an authority on the subject. If the answer is no, this may not be a good source of information.

Objectivity   Every author has a point of view, and some views are more controversial than others. Journalists try to be objective by providing both sides of a story. Academics attempt to persuade readers by presenting a logical argument, which cites other scholars' work. You need to look for two-sided arguments in news and information sites. For academic papers, you need to determine how the paper fits within its discipline and whether the author is using controversial methods for reporting a conclusion.

Authoritative authors situate their work within a larger discipline. This background helps readers evaluate the author's knowledge on a particular subject. You should ascertain whether the author's approach is controversial and whether he or she acknowledges this. More important, is the information being presented as fact or opinion? Authors who argue for their position provide readers with other sources that support their arguments. If no sources are cited, the material may be an opinion piece rather than an objective presentation of information. The following questions can help you determine objectivity:

1. Is the purpose of the site clearly stated, either by the author or the organization authoring the site?
2. Does the site give a balanced viewpoint or present only one side?
3. Is the information directed toward a specific group of viewers?
4. Does the site contain advertising?
5. Does the copyright belong to a person or an organization?
6. Do you see anything to indicate who is funding the site?

Everyone has a point of view. This is important to remember when you are using Web resources. A question to keep asking yourself is, What is the bias or point of view being expressed here?

Coverage   Coverage deals with the breadth and depth of information presented on a Web site. Stated another way, it is about how much information is presented and how detailed the information is. Looking at the site map or index can give you an idea about how much information is contained on a site. This isn't necessarily bad. Coverage is a criteria that is tied closely to your research requirement. For one assignment, a given Web site may be too general for your needs. For another assignment, that same site might be perfect. Some sites contain very little actual information because pages are filled with links to other sites. Coverage also relates to objectivity. You should ask the following questions about coverage:

1. Does the author present both sides of the story or is a piece of the story missing?

2. Is the information comprehensive enough for your needs?
3. Does the site cover too much, too generally?
4. Do you need more specific information than the site can provide?
5. Does the site have an objective approach?

In addition to examining what is covered on a Web site, equally revealing is what is not covered. Missing information can reveal a bias in the material. Keep in mind that you are evaluating the information on a Web site for your research requirements.

Currency   Currency questions deal with the timeliness of information. However, currency is more important for some topics than for others. For example, currency is essential when you are looking for technology related topics and current events. In contrast, currency may not be relevant when you are doing research on Plato or Ancient Greece. In terms of Web sites, currency also pertains to whether the site is being kept up to date and links are being maintained. Sites on the Web are sometimes abandoned by their owners. When people move or change jobs, they may neglect to remove the site from the company or university server. To test currency ask the following questions:

1. Does the site indicate when the content was created?
2. Does the site contain a last revised date? How old is the date? (In the early part of 2001, a university updated their Web site with a "last updated" date of 1901! This obviously was a Y2K problem, but it does point out the need to be observant of such things!)
3. Does the author state how often he or she revises the information? Some sites are on a monthly update cycle (e.g., a government statistics page).
4. Can you tell specifically what content was revised??
5. Is the information still useful for your topic? Even if the last update is old, the site might still be worthy of use if the content is still valid for your research.

Relevancy to Your Research: Primary versus Secondary Sources

Some research assignments require the use of primary (original) sources. Materials such as raw data, diaries, letters, manuscripts, and original accounts of events can be considered primary material. In most cases, these historical documents are no longer copyrighted. The Web is a great source for this type of resource.

Information that has been analyzed and previously interpreted is considered a secondary source. Sometimes secondary sources are more appropriate than primary sources. If, for example, you are asked to analyze a topic or to find an analysis of a topic, a secondary source of an analysis

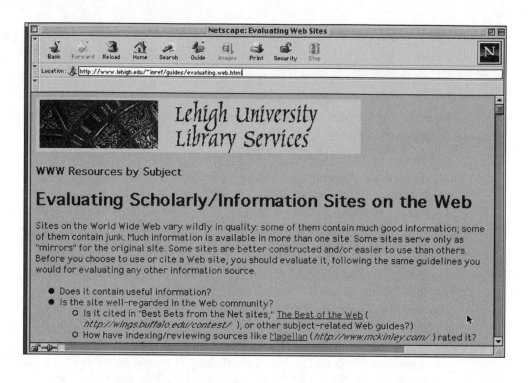

would be most appropriate. Ask yourself the following questions to determine whether the Web site is relevant to your research:

1. Is it a primary or secondary source?
2. Do you need a primary source?
3. Does the assignment require you to cite different types of sources? For example, are you supposed to use at least one book, one journal article, and one Web page?

You need to think critically, both visually and verbally, when evaluating Web sites. Because Web sites are designed as multimedia hypertexts, nonlinear texts, visual elements, and navigational tools are added to the evaluation process.

Help in Evaluating Web Sites   One shortcut to finding high-quality Web sites is using subject directories and meta-sites, which select the Web sites they index by similar evaluation criteria to those just described. If you want to learn more about evaluating Web sites, many colleges and universities provide sites that help you evaluate Web resources. The following list contains some excellent examples of these evaluation sites:

• Evaluating Quality on the Net—Hope Tillman, Babson College
  www.hopetillman.com/findqual.html

- Critical Web Evaluation—Kurt W. Wagner, William Paterson University of New Jersey
euphrates.wpunj.edu/faculty/wagnerk/
- Evaluation Criteria—Susan Beck, New Mexico State University
lib.nmsu.edu/instruction/evalcrit.html
- A Student's Guide to Research with the WWW
www.slu.edu/departments/english/research/
- Evaluating Web Pages: Questions to Ask & Strategies for Getting the Answers
www.lib.berkeley.edu/TeachingLib/Guides/Internet/
EvalQuestions.html

Critical Evaluation Web sites

WEB SITE AND URL	SOURCE
Critical Thinking in an Online World **www.library.ucsb.edu/untangle/ jones.html**	*Paper from "Untangling the Web" 1996*
Educom Review: Information **www.educause.edu/pub/er/review/ reviewArticles/31231.html**	*EDUCAUSE Literacy as a Liberal Art (1996 article)*
Evaluating Information Found on the Internet **MiltonsWeb.mse.jhu.edu/ research/education/net.html**	*University of Utah Library*
Evaluating Web Sites **www.lib.purdue.edu/ StudentInstruction/ evaluating_web_sites.html**	*Purdue University Library*
Evaluating Web Sites **www.lehigh.edu/~inref/guides/ evaluating.web.html**	*Lehigh University*
ICONnect: Curriculum Connections Overview **www.ala.org/ICONN/evaluate.html**	*American Library Association's technology education initiative*
Kathy Schrock's ABC's of Web Site Evaluation **www.kathyschrock.net/abceval/**	*Author's Web site*
Kids Pick the best of the Web "Top 10: Announced" **www.ala.org/news/topkidpicks.html**	*American Library Association initiative underwritten by Microsoft (1998)*

Resource Selection and Inofmration
Evaluation
**alexia.lis.uiuc.edu/~janicke/
Evaluate.html**

*Univ of Illinois, Champaign-
Urbana (Librarian)*

Testing the Surf: Criteria for Evaluating
Internet Information Sources
**info.lib.uh.edu/pr/v8/n3/
smit8n3.html**

University of Houston Libraries

Evaluating Web Resources
**muse.widener.edu/
Wolfgram-Memorial-Library/
webevaluation/webeval.htm**

Widener University Library

UCLA College Library Instruction:
Thinking Critically about World
Wide Web Resources
**www.library.ucla.edu/libraries/
college/help/critical/**

UCLA Library

UG OOL: Judging Quality on
the Internet
**www.open.uoguelph.ca/
resources/skills/judging.html**

University of Guelph

Web Evaluation Criteria
**lib.nmsu.edu/instruction/
evalcrit.html**

*New Mexico State University
Library*

Web Page Credibility Checklist
**www.park.pvt.k12.md.us/
academics/research/credcheck.htm**

Park School of Baltimore

Evaluating Websites for Educational
Uses: Bibliography and Checklist
www.unc.edu/cit/guides/irg-49.html

University of North Carolina

Evaluating Web Sites
**www.lesley.edu/library/guides/
research/evaluating_web.html**

Lesley University

> *TIP:* Can't seem to get a URL to work? If the URL doesn't begin with www,
> you may need to put the http:// in front of the URL. Usually, browsers can
> handle URLs that begin with www without the need to type in the "http://"
> but if you find you're having trouble, add the http://.

Documentation Guidelines for Online Sources

MLA Documentation of Electronic Sources

This section illustrates the new guidelines for electronic sources included in the recently published second edition of the *MLA Style Manual and Guide to Scholarly Publishing* (New York: MLA, 1998). For additional information about the MLA's new style manual, see *MLA on the Web* <http://www.mla.org/>, a site that is also useful for its list of frequently asked questions about MLA style.

Electronic texts appear in a variety of forms, and new ones appear with some frequency. Many electronic texts have print counterparts (e.g., newspaper and journal articles), and the examples that follow show how the MLA has adapted older forms to accommodate these new media. At times, it may be necessary to improvise in the same spirit. As in documenting any source, the most important function of the citation is to allow readers to locate that text for themselves. For that reason, keep the following guidelines in mind:

- Use the whole uniform resource locator (URL), beginning with the mode of access (e.g., *http*, *FTP*, *Gopher*) and including all the extensions following the first single slash mark. Be sure to check this portion of the entry for accuracy. If you are able to move back and forth between the online source you are reading and a document you are creating, you might consider copying the URL and pasting it in the document to ensure accuracy.
- Provide as much of the requested information as is available. It will often be necessary to look at several pages of a Web document to find such things as the organization sponsoring the Web page or the date of the latest version. When a piece of information is not available (and sometimes it is not), then go on to the next item.
- Give the date of access as well as the date of publication given in the document. Because electronic texts can be revised easily and revision dates are not always given, there is no guarantee that the text a writer cites will be the one a reader retrieves. The date of access helps to account for any differences that may occur.
- If it is necessary to divide a URL between lines in your works cited entry, divide it only after a slash mark. Neither a hyphen nor any other character should be used to indicate the division.

Note: Dividing the URL only after a slash may result in some odd-looking citations. The date of access and the URL should begin on the same line and are not separated by any punctuation. In some cases, a URL divided at the slash mark may begin on the next line instead; in other cases, the line lengths will be noticeably uneven.

This guide is organized like the new *MLA Style Manual* by grouping electronic resources into five large categories: online scholarly projects, reference databases, and personal or professional sites; online books; articles in online periodicals; CD-ROMs; and other electronic sources (e.g., advertising, e-mail). It also suggests formats for commercial online services (such as CompuServe, Dialog, or America Online) that are not clearly covered by the new style manual.

An Online Scholarly Project, Reference Database, or Professional or Personal Site

An entry for an entire online scholarly project or database should contain the following elements:

1. Title of the project or database (underlined)
2. Name of the editor or director of the project or database (if given)
3. Electronic publication information, including version number, date of electronic publication or latest update, and name of sponsoring institution or organization
4. Date of access and electronic address (the latter in angle brackets)

The first group of examples illustrates how to cite an entire online scholarly project or reference database.

American Verse Project. 16 Oct. 1996. University of
    Michigan and Humanities Text Initiative. 15 June
    1998 <http://www.hti.umich.edu/english/amverse/>.

Microsoft Encarta Concise Encyclopedia. 1998.
    Microsoft. 15 June 1998 <http://encarta.msn.com/
    find/find.asp>.

Paul Laurence Dunbar digital Text Archives. 1992.
    Wright State U. 15 June 1998
    <http://www.libraries.wright.edu/dunbar/>.

The Perseus Project. Ed. Gregory R. Crane. Mar.
    1997. Dept. of Classics, Tufts U. 15 June 1998
    <http://www.perseus.tufts.edu/>.

Project Gutenberg. Ed. Michael S. Hart. 1998.
    Illinois Benedictine College. 15 June 1998
    <http://www.promo.net/pg/>.

It is much more common to use only a portion of a scholarly project or database. To cite an essay, poem, or other short work, begin with the author's name, followed by the title of the work within quotation marks, and the full information for the project. If the URL for the short work differs from that of the project, use the URL of the short work. As the following illustrations show, the difference can be considerable.

```
Martin, Thomas. "Overview of Archaic and Classical
    Greek History." The Perseus Project. Ed. Gregory
    R. Crane. Mar. 1997. Dept. of Classics, Tufts U.
    15 June 1998 <http://hydra.perseus.tufts.edu/
    cgi-bin/text?lookup=trm+ov+toc>.

Wilde, Oscar. "Helas!" Project Gutenberg. Ed. Michael
    S. Hart. Oct. 1997. Illinois Benedictine College.
    15 June 1998 <ftp://uiarchive.cso.uiuc.edu/pub/
    etext/gutenberg/etext97/pmwld10.txt>.
```

To cite an anonymous article within a reference database, begin with the name of the article (in quotation marks) and then provide the rest of the information for the database. If the URL for the article differs from that of the whole database, use the URL of the article, as in the following illustrations.

```
"Loch Ness Monster." Encyclopedia Smithsonian. 1994.
    Smithsonian Institution. 15 June 1998 <http://
    www.si.edu/resource/faq/nmnh/lochness.htm>.

"Nike." The Perseus Project. Ed. Gregory R. Crane.
    Mar. 1997. Dept. of Classics, Tufts U. 15 June
    1998 <http://www.perseus.tufts.edu/cgi-bin/
    lookup?lookup=nike>.
```

In addition to scholarly projects and reference databases, the new *MLA Style Manual* identifies two other types of Web sites, professional and personal. The *MLA on the Web* entry on page 22 demonstrates the first category, and the home page of Paul Brians illustrates the second. Also included are some Web sites that do not fit clearly into either category. *The Margaret Atwood Information Web Site* combines the two categories; although it is the Canadian author's own Web site, it is maintained on her behalf by a number of other people. Still other Web sites might be thought of as "commercial" sites, since they are maintained by companies but are really not advertisements in the usual sense. The illustration drawn from the the Levi Strauss Web site demonstrates how such information might be documented.

iSearch: English

Atwood, Margaret. <u>The Margaret Atwood Information Web Site</u>. 15 June 1998 <http://www.web.net/owtoad>.

<u>The Atwood Society's Margaret Atwood Information Site</u>. 19 May 1998. The Margaret Atwood Society and Thomas B. Friedman. 15 June 1998 <http://www.cariboo.bc.ca/atwood/>.

Brians, Paul. Home page. 16 June 1997 <http://www.wsu.edu:8080/~brians/index.html>.

"The History of Levi's 501 Jeans." <u>Levi Strauss.com</u>. 1997. 18 June 1998 <http://www.levistrauss.com/lsc_history_501.html>.

<u>MLA on the Web</u>. 1997. 15 June 1998 <http://www.mla.org/>.

An Online Book

Online books may be part of a scholarly project or published independently. The citation for an independently published book should contain the following items:

1. Author's name. If only an editor, compiler, or translator is identified, cite that name, followed by the appropriate abbreviation (*ed., comp., trans.*)
2. Title of the work (underlined)
3. Name of the editor, compiler, or translator
4. Publication information. If the online version has not been published before, give the date of electronic publication and the name of any sponsoring institution or organization. State the publication facts about the original print version if they are given; you may use square brackets to add relevant information not provided in the source
5. Date of access and electronic address (the latter in angle brackets)

Dickens, Charles. <u>The Cricket on the Hearth</u>. [1846]. 16 June 1998 <ftp://ftp.books.com/ebooks/Fiction/Authors/D/Dickens/CRICKET.TXT>.

Stork, David G., ed. <u>Hal's Legacy: 2001's Computer as Dream and Reality</u>. Cambridge: MIT P, 1996. 16 June 1998 <http://mitpress.mit.edu/e-books/Hal/>.

iSearch: English

Turgenev, Ivan. <u>Fathers and Sons</u>. 1861. Trans.
  Richard Hare. [London]: Hutchinson, 1948. 16 June
  1998 <http://eldred.ne.mediaone.net/ist/fas.htm>.

To cite a book that is part of a scholarly project, provide the relevant information from the five items outlined above, followed by publication information for the project. If the URL of the book and the project differ, use the URL of the book.

Austen, Jane. <u>Emma</u>. <u>Project Gutenberg</u>. Ed. Michael
  S. Hart. Aug. 1994. Illinois Benedictine College.
  15 June 1998 <ftp://uiarchive.cso.uiuc.edu/pub/
  etext/gutenberg/etext94/emma10.txt>.

Dunbar, Paul Laurence. <u>Lyrics of Lowly Life</u>. New
  York: Dodd, 1896. <u>Paul Laurence Dunbar Digital
  Archives</u>. 1992. Wright State U. 15 June 1998
  <http://www.library.wright.edu/dunbar/
  lowly1.html#Contents17>.

To cite part of an online book, place the title or name of the part between the author's name and the title of the book. Punctuate the title of the part of the book as you would if it were in print (e.g., the title of an essay or poem would be in quotation marks, but a preface or introduction would have no special punctuation). If the URLs of the book and the portion you are citing differ, include the URL of the part you are using. The two illustrations cite different portions of the same online book.

Dunbar, Paul Laurence. "An Ante-Bellum Sermon."
  <u>Lyrics of Lowly Life</u>. New York: Dodd, 1896.
  <u>Paul Laurence Dunbar Digital Text Archives</u>.
  1992. Wright State U. 15 June 1998 <http://
  www.libraries.wright.edu/dunbar/
  lowly2.html#lowly18>.

Howells, William Dean. Introduction. <u>Lyrics of
  Lowly Life</u>. By Paul Laurence Dunbar. New York:
  Dodd, 1896. <u>Paul Laurence Dunbar Digital Text
  Archives</u>. 1992. Wright State U. 15 June 1998
  <http://www.library.wright.edu/dunbar/
  lowly1.html#Contents58>.

An Article in an Online Periodical

Online periodicals fit into much the same categories as their print counterparts—scholarly journals, newspapers, magazines—and the forms for citing them are similar. The citation should contain the following elements:

1. Author's name
2. Title of the work or material (in quotation marks). (If a review or letter to the editor is unnamed, use the appropriate descriptive term—e.g., *letter*—without quotation marks.)
3. Name of the periodical (underlined)
4. Volume number, issue number, or other identifying number
5. Date of publication
6. The number range or total number of pages, paragraphs, or other sections, if numbered
7. Date of access and electronic address (the latter in angle brackets)

a. An Article in a Scholarly Journal

Best, Michael. "From Book to Screen: A Window on Renaissance Electronic Texts." <u>Early Modern Literary Studies</u> 1.2 (1995): 27 pars. 17 June 1998 <http://purl.oclc.org/emls/01-2/ bestbook.html>.

Chiel, Hillel J. "Critical Thinking in a Neurobiology Course." <u>Bioscene</u> 22 (1996): 13 pp. 17 June 1998 <http://papa.indstate.edu/amcbt/ volume_22/v22n1s3.html>.

George, Pamela G. "The Effectiveness of Cooperative Learning Strategies in Multicultural University Classrooms." <u>Journal on Excellence in College Teaching</u> 5.1 (1994): 21–30. 16 June 1998 <http://www.lib.muohio.edu/ject/html/v5n1/ v5n1-George.html>.

Hubona, Geoffrey S., Gregory W. Shirah, and David G. Fout. "The Effect of Motion and Stereopsis on Three-Dimensional Visualization." <u>International Journal of Human-Computer Studies</u> 4 (1997): 609–27. 16 June 1998 <http://fai.idealibrary.com:80/ cgi-bin/fai.idealibrary.com_8100/ class;Cfmedia::CMDApplication;deliver/ 0100015f040402000f060d02015f01060508/ 130:1121:58319/article.pdf>.

b. An Article in a Newspaper or on a Newswire

"Au Pair's Hometown Cheers Ruling." <u>AP Online</u> 16
    June 1998. 16 June 1998 <http://www.nytimes.com/
    aponline/I/AP-Britain-Au-Pair-Reaction.html>.

Griffiths, Paul. "Looking for Love in Bizet's
    Highland Fling." <u>New York Times</u> 29 June 1998.
    Electronic. America Online. 29 June 1998.

King, Sharon R. "Monday's Stocks: U.S. Stocks Plunge
    as Asian Turmoil Worsens." <u>New York Times on the Web</u>
    16 June 1998. 16 June 1998 <http://www.nytimes.com/
    yr/mo/day/news/financial/market.html>.

(**Note:** The Griffiths article was obtained through a commercial online service that does not use a URL. See pages 30–31 for a more detailed explanation about documenting such sources.)

c. An Article in a Magazine

Caldwell, Christopher. "The Southern Captivity of
    the GOP." <u>Atlantic Monthly</u> June 1998: 55–72. 16
    June 1998 <http://www.theatlantic.com/issues/
    current/gop.htm>.

Jellinek, George. "Bryn Terfel Sings Heroic Handel
    Arias." <u>Stereo Review</u> Apr. 1998. Electronic.
    America Online. 29 June 1998.

Johnson, Roy S. "The Jordan Effect." <u>Fortune</u> 22 June
    1998. 16 June 1998 <http://www.pathfinder.com/
    fortune/1998/980622/jor.html>.

Stone, Peter S. "The Nicotine Network." <u>Mother
    Jones</u> May–June 1996. 16 June 1998 <http://
    www.mojones.com/mother_jones/MJ96/stone2.html>.

(**Notes:** The Jellinek article was obtained through a commercial online service that does not use a URL. See pages 30–31 for a more detailed explanation about documenting such sources. The dates in the third illustration above really are correct. The story about Michael Jordan was available online several days earlier than the publication date that appears on the cover of the magazine.)

d. A Review

Rodger, Blake. Rev. of <u>Milton's Imperial Epic:
Paradise Lost and the Discourse of Colonialism</u>,
by Martin Evans. <u>Milton Review</u> 13 (1998). 16 June
1998. <http://www.richmond.edu/~creamer/
mr13.html>.

Schickel, Richard. "Childhood Nightmares." Rev. of
<u>The Butcher Boy</u>, dir. Neil Jordan. <u>Time</u> 6 Apr.
1998. 17 June 1998 <http://www.pathfinder.com/
time/magazine/1998/dom/980406/
the_arts.cinema.childhoo18.html>.

e. An Abstract

Hubona, Geoffrey S., Gregory W. Shirah, and David G.
Fout. "The Effect of Motion and Stereopsis on
Three-Dimensional Visualization." <u>International
Journal of Human-Computer Studies</u> 4 (1997):
609–27. Abstract. 16 June 1998
<http://fai.idealibrary.com:80/
cgi-bin/fai.idealibrary.com_8100/fetch/
0100015f040402020f070701035703050f03/
130:1123:4203/0>.

f. An Editorial

"Michael's Last Hurrah?" Editorial. <u>New York Times
on the Web</u> 16 June 1998. 15 June 1998 <http://
www.nytimes.com/yr/mo/day/editorial/16tue3.html>.

Smith, Harriet. Editorial. <u>International Piano
Quarterly</u> Winter 1998. 15 June 1998 <http://
www.gramophone.co.uk/i.html>.

g. A Letter to the Editor

Montague, Paul. Letter. <u>Time</u> 23 Mar. 1998. 17 June
1998 <http://www.pathfinder.com/time/magazine/
1998/dom/980323/letters.letters.28.html>.

iSearch: English

Publications on CD-ROM, Diskette, or Magnetic Tape

Many texts appear in several formats, such as print, CD-ROM, diskette, or magnetic tape. The forms for electronic versions of these sources are similar to their print counterparts. The MLA divides these sources into two categories—nonperiodical publications and periodical publications. The first kind is published as a book would be; that is, published once, without any plan for updates. The second kind is published on a regular schedule, like a journal or magazine.

The entry for a nonperiodical publication on CD-ROM, diskette, or magnetic tape consists of the following items:

1. Author's name (if given). If the name of an editor, compiler, or translator is given instead, cite that person's name, followed by the appropriate abbreviation (*ed., comp., trans.*)
2. Title of the publication (underlined)
3. Name of editor, compiler, or translator (if relevant)
4. Publication medium (*CD-ROM, Diskette,* or *Magnetic tape*)
5. Edition, release, or version (if relevant), using the appropriate abbreviation (*Ed., Rel., Vers.*)
6. Place of publication
7. Name of publisher
8. Date of publication

The date of access is not included because these media cannot be revised in the same way that online publications can. The first examples below demonstrate how to cite an entire work on CD-ROM. An entry for a diskette or magnetic tape would be done in the same way, with only the medium changed. If some of the information is not provided, cite whatever is available. (In the second illustration, neither the CD-ROM nor the material accompanying it is dated.)

Ingpen, Robert, and Philip Wilkinson. <u>Ideas That Changed the World</u>. CD-ROM. Toronto: ICE Integrated Communications and Entertainment, 1996.

<u>World's Greatest Speeches</u>. CD-ROM. Irvine: Softbit, n.d.

If publication information for a printed version is provided, begin the citation with that information.

Coleridge, Samuel Taylor. <u>The Complete Works of Samuel Taylor Coleridge</u>. Ed. Ernest Hartley Coleridge. 2 vols. Oxford: Clarendon, 1912. <u>English Poetry Full-Text Database</u>. Rel. 2. CD-ROM. Cambridge, Eng.: Chadwyck, 1993.

iSearch: English

If you are citing only part of a work, identify the part and punctuate the title appropriately (e.g., underline the title of a book-length work or use quotation marks for an article, poem, or short story). If the source provides numbers for pages, paragraphs, screens, or some other division, include that information.

Bryan, William Jennings. "The Cross of Gold."
    World's Greatest Speeches. CD-ROM. Irvine:
    Softbit, n.d.

Coleridge, Samuel Taylor. "An Ode to the Rain." The
    Complete Works of Samuel Taylor Coleridge. Ed.
    Ernest Hartley Coleridge. Vol. 1. Oxford:
    Clarendon, 1912. 382–84. English Poetry Full-Text
    Database. Rel. 2. CD-ROM. Cambridge, Eng.:
    Chadwyck, 1993.

Ingpen, Robert, and Philip Wilkinson. "Babbage's
    Machines." Ideas That Changed the World. CD-ROM.
    Toronto: ICE Integrated Communications and
    Entertainment, 1996.

The form for citing CD-ROMs that are published periodically is similar to that for nonperiodical publications. It contains the following items:

1. Author's name (if given)
2. Publication information for any identified printed source or analogue
3. Title of the database (underlined)
4. Publication medium
5. Name of the vendor (if relevant). (Some information providers lease their data to vendors, such as SilverPlatter or UMI-ProQuest, rather than publishing it themselves.)
6. Electronic publication date

Once again, the date of access is not required. The first example below illustrates how to document a portion of a work published periodically in one of these media. The second illustrates how to document the whole work.

Trail, George Y. "Teaching Argument and the Rhetoric
    of Orwell's 'Politics and the English Language.'"
    College English 57 (1995): 570–83. Abstract.
    ERIC. CD-ROM. SilverPlatter. Sept. 1996.

United States. Dept. of Commerce. Bureau of the
    Census. U.S. Imports of Merchandise. CD-ROM. Data
    User Services Division. Mar. 1994.

iSearch: English

Other Electronic Sources

In addition to the electronic sources described above, MLA provides guidelines for a number of other media.

a. A Television or Radio Program

Caplan, Jeff. "The Best Way to Put Out a Hit on
   Mosquitos." <u>Healthy Living</u>. CBS Radio. WCBS, New
   York, 16 June 1998. Transcript. 17 June 1998
   <http://www.newsradio88.com/health/history/
   june_1998/june_16.html>.

b. A Sound Recording or Sound Clip

Schumann, Robert. "Arabesque." <u>The Romantic Piano</u>.
   WCLV, 1997. 17 June 1998 <http://www.wclv.com/
   sounds/arabesk.mp2>.

c. A Film or Film Clip

Softley, Iain, dir. <u>The Wings of the Dove</u>. Miramax,
   1997. 18 June 1998 <http://www.hollywood.com/
   trailers/wingsdove/high_wingsdove.ram>.

d. A Work of Art

Simmons, John. <u>Titania</u>. 1866. Bristol Museums and
   Art Gallery. 17 June 1998 <http://
   www.nextcity. com/go/ago/>.

van Gogh, Vincent. <u>The Starry Night</u>. 1889. Museum
   of Modern Art, New York. 16 June 1998 <http://
   www.moma.org/collection/paintsculpt/
   vangogh.starry.html>.

e. An Interview

Atwood, Margaret. Interview with Marilyn Snell.
   <u>Mother Jones</u> July-Aug. 1997. 18 June 1998
   <http://www.motherjones.com/mother_jones/JA97/
   visions.html>.

f. A Map

"Hobart, Oklahoma." Map. <u>U.S. Gazetteer</u>. US Census
   Bureau. 17 June 1998 <http://www.census.gov/
   cgi-bin/gazetteer?city=Hobart&state=OK&zip=>.

g. A Cartoon

Stossel, Sage. "Even Better Than Viagra." Cartoon.
<u>Atlantic Monthly</u> 20 May 1998. 29 June 1998
<http://www2.theAtlantic.com/atlantic/unbound/
sage/ss980520.htm>.

h. An Advertisement

Toyota Land Cruiser. Advertisement. 17 June
1998 <http://www.toyota.com/
welcome@SK@0rY0z11f27T1C@@.html>.

i. A Manuscript or Working Paper

Davis, George K., and Bryce E. Kanago. "The
Correlation Between Prices and Output:
Controlling for Contaminating Dynamics." Working
paper, n.d. <http://www.sba.muohio.edu/davisgk/
Research/pycor.pdf>.

Whitman, Walt. "Live Oak, with Moss." Ms. Valentine-
Barrett Collection. University of Virginia. 17
June 1998 <http://jefferson.village.virginia.edu/
whitman/manscripts/moss/oak1.html>.

j. An E-mail Communication   To cite e-mail sent to an individual,
give the name of the writer, the title of the message (the subject line) in
quotation marks, a description that includes the name of the recipient, and
the date the message was sent. In the first example, the word *author* refers
to the person writing the paper in which the e-mail message is being cited.

Smith, Ray. "Re: Pride and Prejudice Adaptations."
E-mail to the author. 1 July 1998.

Willis, Jonathan. E-mail to Margaret Taylor. 28 June
1998.

k. An Online Posting   Citing e-mail posted to a discussion list calls for
more detailed information. It should provide the name of the author, the
title of the message (the subject line) in quotation marks, a description
(*Online posting*), the date the message was posted, the name of the discussion list, the date of access, and the Internet site or e-mail address of
the list in angle brackets. The form will be the same whether you are citing an e-mail list (the Williams example), a World Wide Web forum (Roth),
or a Usenet newsgroup (Lamming). Whenever possible, cite an archived

copy of the message, which is easier for readers to retrieve. The Curtis example below is an archival version rather than the initial posting.

Curtis, Richard. "Group Dynamnics Training for
    Leaders." Online posting. 12 Nov. 1993.
    Wildornt Discussion Group. 1 July 1998 <gopher://
    lists.Princeton.EDU:70/0R8935-9654-/wildornt/
    logs/log9311>.

Lamming, Andrew. "Faroe-ese??" Online posting.
    23 June 1998. 29 June 1998
    <news:comp.edu.languages.natural>.

Roth, Kevin. Online posting. 30 Oct. 1997. Athletes
    Behaving Badly. 29 June 1998 <http://
    forums.nytimes.com/webin/WebX?13@^9878@.ee9a6af/0>.

Williams, Angela. "Re: Tutor Certification." Online
    posting. 16 June 1998. WAC-L. 18 June 1998
    <wac-1@postoffice.cso.uiuc.edu>.

If you want to cite a document that has been forwarded as part of another posting, begin with the name of the writer, the title, and the date of the original document. Continue with the name of the person who forwarded that posting and then provide the appropriate information for the posting in which the document was forwarded. The illustration below refers to Richard Curtis's original message (illustrated above) that was forwarded in Sandy Kohn's message.

Curtis, Richard. "Group Dynamics Training for
    Leaders." 12 Nov. 1993. Fwd. By Sandy Kohn.
    Online posting. 15 Nov. 1993. Wildornt
    Discussion Group. 1 July 1998 <gopher://
    lists.Princeton.EDU:70/0R9654-10956-/
    wildornt/logs/log9311>.

l. A Synchronous Communication To cite a communication that took place in a MUD (multiuser domain) or MOO (multiuser domain, object-oriented), give the name of the speaker (if you cite only one), a description of the event, the date of the event, the forum for the event (MiamiMoo and LinguaMOO in the examples that follow), and the address. If you cite more than one speaker, begin with the description of the event. If the event has been archived, cite that version so that readers can consult it. The first example below illustrates an archived version of a single paper presented at an online conference that took place on a MOO; the second illustrates how to cite the entire conference. The final illustration demonstrates how to cite an individual exchange that took place on a MOO.

Haynes-Burton, Cynthia. Online conference
    presentation. "Writing and Community: The Use of
    MOOs in the Teaching of Writing." "Text-Based
    Virtual Reality: What Is It and How Is It Being
    Used?" Online conference. 11 Oct. 1994. LinguaMOO.
    18 June 1998 <http://www.utdallas.edu/~cynthiah/
    lingua_archive/meridian-moo-seminar.txt>.

"Text-Based Virtual Reality: What Is It and How Is
    It Being Used?" Online conference. 11 Oct. 1994.
    LinguaMOO. 18 June 1998 <http://www.utdallas.edu/
    ~cynthiah/lingua_archive/
    meridian-moo-seminar.txt>.

Wallrodt, Susan. Online discussion of virtual Delphi
    site. 18 June 1998. MiamiMoo. 18 June 1998
    <telnet://moo.cas.muohio.edu>.

Sources from a Commercial Online Service

The new *MLA Style Manual* says nothing about how to cite materials provided by a commercial service, such as CompuServe or America Online. In many cases, there is no need for a special citation form. For example, anyone using one of these services to access sites on the World Wide Web will have the URL and other necessary information at hand and can simply follow the MLA format for Web sites. However, some sources of information are available only to those who subscribe to that service. Until the MLA develops a specific form for citing commercial services, the best course is probably to supply the information that would be needed for a reader to locate that source. The following examples demonstrate how to document such sources in ways consistent with MLA style. Like the other forms, these begin with the name of the author, the title of the work, and the date it was posted or updated. The word *Electronic* is used to identify the medium, the name of the service follows, and the citation ends with the date of access.

Dunbar, William. "Lament for the Makaris Quhen He
    Was Sek." Representative Poetry On-Line. U of
    Toronto P, 1996. Rep. Poetry 2RP1.55. Electronic.
    America Online. 24 June 1998.

"Censorship." <u>Merriam-Webster Dictionary</u>. 1998 ed. Electronic. America Online. 30 June 1998.

Griffiths, Paul. "Looking for Love in Bizet's Highland Fling." <u>New York Times</u> 29 June 1998. Electronic. America Online. 29 June 1998.

Jellinek, George. "Bryn Terfel Sings Heroic Handel Arias." <u>Stereo Review</u> Apr. 1998. Electronic. America Online. 29 June 1998.

"Run with It." Bob's Fitness Tips. Oprah Online. 29 Jan. 1998. Electronic. America Online. 24 June 1998.

Citing Electronic Sources in the Text

In principle, electronic sources are cited the same way as print sources in the body of a paper. For citing an entire work, only the name of the author (or the title, if no author is identified) is required. Quoting, paraphrasing, or otherwise referring to a specific passage in a printed source calls for the author's name (or the title, if no author is identified) and a page number. If an electronic source contains page, paragraph, or screen numbers, they can be used. With page numbers, use only the author's name and the page number, as when citing a print source; with paragraph or screen numbers, use the author's name, followed by a comma, and the abbreviation *par.* or the word *screen* in addition to the number. If there are no numbers, use only the author's name (or the title, if no author is idenfitied). The following illustrations are drawn from the examples used earlier.

Citing an Entire Work

Although Michael Jordan's economic impact on basketball has been enormous, it cannot be measured in simple terms (Johnson).

or

As Roy S. Johnson points out, Michael Jordan's economic impact on basketball has been enormous, but it cannot be measured in simple terms.

Citing Part of a Work

Document with page numbers

George Davis and Bryce Kanago suggest that recessions can be generated by large supply

iSearch: English

iSearch: English

shocks, large demand shocks, or a combination of both (12).

or

Economists at Miami University suggest that recessions can be generated by large supply shocks, large demand shocks, or a combination of both (Davis and Kanago 12).

Document with numbered paragraphs

Michael Best warns that trying to make online books seem like printed books may lead to seeing the screen simply as "a poor imitation of the original book" (par. 1).

or

The effort to make online books seem like printed books may lead to seeing the screen simply as "a poor imitation of the original book." (Best, par. 1).

Document without page, paragraph, or screen numbers

Paul Montague is skeptical of the agreement reached between UN Secretary-General Kofi Annan and Saddam Hussein, reminding readers of British Prime Minister Neville Chamberlain's 1938 meeting with Hitler and the 1939 invasion of Poland.

APA Documentation of Electronic Sources

The fifth edition of the *Publication Manual of the American Psychological Association* addresses how to document electronic sources and other non-print media in a variety of situations. Following are examples of the most commonly used citations.

Electronic Sources

1. General Guidelines for Citing URLs in the Reference List
   - Dividing URLs

Divide a URL only after a slash or before a period. The following example illustrates both:

```
Schino, G. (2001). Grooming, competition, and social
    rank among female primates: A meta-analysis.
    Animal Behavior, 62, 265-271. Retrieved
    September 27, 2001, from http://
    www.idealibrary.com/links/doi/10.1006/anbe
    .2001.1750/pdf
```

- Punctuating URLs

    There is no period after a URL at the end of a citation so that readers will not think the period is part of the URL.

- Providing Retrieval Dates

The APA *Publication Manual* instructs writers to provide retrieval dates for electronic media when it seems likely that the document may have been altered from a print equivalent or may be modified after it has been posted. Thus, including the retrieval date is a judgment call; if you are in doubt, it is probably best to include it, as shown below:

```
Animal intelligence. (1999). Retrieved September 28,
    2001, from http://www.pethelp.net/cognit.html
```

2. General Guidelines for In-Text Citations of Internet or Other Electronic Sources

To cite an Internet document in the body of a paper, provide the name of the author, followed by the date. If no author is given, begin with the name of the document. If the reference is to a particular portion of the document—such as a direct quotation—provide the additional information needed to help the reader locate it.

If the document has page numbers, the citation looks like this:

```
(Schino, 2001, p. 267)
```

If the paragraphs are numbered, the citation is done in this way:

```
(Knox, 2001, ¶5)
```

or

```
(Knox, 2001, para. 5)  if the paragraph symbol is not
available.
```

If the document contains no page or paragraph numbers, provide the author's name (or the name of the document if no author is identified) and the date:

(<u>Animal Intelligence</u>, 1999)

Readers can easily search most documents for the specific passage that has been quoted.

3. Specific Citation Guidelines

A. An Online Book

The APA *Publication Manual* provides no illustration for online books. When APA develops a format, it will probably be posted on its Web site (http://www.apastyle.org/elecref.html). Until then, a sensible approach would be to combine the relevant elements of the appropriate book entry and electronic forms. For instance, if the online version reproduces the text exactly, it might take this form:

```
Meyer, C. L. (1997). The wandering uterus: Politics
    and the reproductive rights of women [Electronic
    version]. New York: New York University Press.
```

If it is likely that the text has been altered in its electronic version, the reference might take this form:

```
Meyer, C. L. (1997). The wandering uterus: Politics
    and the reproductive rights of women. New York:
    New York University Press. Retrieved October 3,
    2001, from http://emedia.netlibrary.com
```

B. An Article in an Online Publication with a Print Equivalent

- If the online publication exactly duplicates the print version, simply add the description [Electronic version] after the title of the article:

```
Schino, G. (2001). Grooming, competition, and social
    rank among female primates: A meta-analysis.
    [Electronic version]. Animal Behavior, 62,
    265-271.
```

- If you have reason to believe the text has changed in some way (e.g., page numbers have been omitted or information has been updated), add the date you retrieved the item and the URL:

```
Schino, G. (2001). Grooming, competition, and social
    rank among female primates: A meta-analysis.
```

<u>Animal Behavior</u>, 62, 265–271. Retrieved September
27, 2001, from http://www.idealibrary.com/links/
doi/10.1006/anbe.2001.1750/pdf

C. An Article in an Online Journal or Magazine Without Print Equivalent

Knox, S. L. (2001, May). The productive power of
confessions of cruelty. <u>Postmodern Culture</u>,
11(3). Retrieved September 21, 2001, from
http://www.iath.virginia.edu/pmc/current.issue/
11.3knox.html

D. An Article in an Online Newspaper

Sandomir, R. (2001, September 21). Football, set for
TV return, is benching its war clichés. <u>The New
York Times</u>. Retrieved September 21, 2001, from
http://www.nytimes.com/2001/09/21/sports/
football/21LANG.html

E. An Article Retrieved from a Database

Brown, S. P., Ganesan, S., & Challagalla, G. (2001).
Self-efficacy as a moderator of information-
seeking effectiveness. <u>Journal of Applied
Psychology</u>, 86, 1043–1051. Retrieved October 13,
2001, from PsychINFO database.

F. An Individual Section of an Internet Document

Benton Foundation. (1999, May 3). Barriers. In
<u>Networking for better care: Health care in the
information age</u> (chap. 2). Retrieved September
24, 2001, from http://www.benton.org/Library/
health/two.htm

G. A Complete Internet Document

• When the author of a sponsoring organization is named:

Benton Foundation. (1999, May 3). <u>Networking for
better care: Health care in the information age</u>.
Retrieved September 24, 2001, from http://
www.benton.org

- When the author or organization is not named:

<u>Animal intelligence</u>. (1999). Retrieved September 28,
    2001, from http://www.pethelp.net/cognit.html

H. Personal E-mail and Other Forms of Personal Communication

Because personal e-mail cannot be retrieved by the reader of the paper,
it is not included in the reference list at the end of the paper. It is cited
in the body of the paper, in this form: (B. J. Lawson, personal
communication, September 26, 2001). The same wording is
used for personal letters, memos, personal interviews, and telephone
conversations.

I. A Message Posted to a Newsgroup

Messages that can be retrieved by the reader—such as those posted to a
newsgroup, discussion list, online forum, and the like—should be included
in the reference list. The entry would take this form:

Williams, W. E. (2001, September 20). Killing the
    messenger [Msg 2384]. Message posted to
    http://forums.nytimes.com/webin/WebX?13@@.efe8124

Other Non-Print Media

1. Motion Pictures and Videotapes

APA uses the term *motion picture* to describe film available on videotape
as well as film shown in a theater. For both, give the name and, in parentheses, the function of the primary contributors to the work (the director
or producer or both). The APA manual does not include a period at the end
of any of the film entries.

For Widely Distributed Commercial Films:

Scorsese, M. (Director), & Chartoff, R. (Producer).
    (1980). <u>Raging bull</u> [Motion picture]. United
    States: Metro-Goldwyn-Mayer Pictures

iSearch: English

For Films with Limited Availability:

American Psychological Association (Producer).
   (1997). <u>Cognitive therapy for panic disorders</u>
   [Motion picture]. (Available from the American
   Psychological Association, 750 First Street, NE,
   Washington, DC 20002-4242)

Note that this citation specifies where the film can be obtained, including city name.

2. Television Broadcasts

Crystal, L. (Executive producer). (2001, September
   28). <u>The news hour with Jim Lehrer</u> [Television
   broadcast]. New York and Washington, DC: Public
   Broadcasting Service.

3. Audio Recordings

For citing audio in text, identify the artist, date, and track number: (Benjamin, 1988, track 5). The formats for reference list citations follow.

When the Music is Performed by the Writer:

Benjamin, T. C. (1988). Domesticity blues. On <u>An
   urban legend in his own time</u> [CD]. Akron, OH:
   Do-Gooder Recordings.

When the Music is Performed by an Artist Other than the Writer:

Benjamin, T. C. (1988). Domesticity blues [Recorded
   by G. White & R. Vestas]. On <u>Songs of modern
   life</u> [CD]. Columbus, OH: Capital Recordings.
   (2001)

The date in parentheses at the end is the date of the recording by White and Vestas; it is not followed by a period.

iSearch: English

Web Activities

Internet Activities for College English

1. Find an e-mail discussion list (listserv) that you might be interested in. Lurk for a week or two. Can you find its FAQ? How would you characterize the tone of most of the postings? Are controversial issues tackled? Are there any flames? If so, for what reason? What seems to be a significant taboo on this list?

2. Do the same for a Usenet newsgroup. What are the differences you see between the newsgroup and the e-mail list?

3. If anyone seems particularly knowledgeable or authoritative on either the list or the newsgroup, after a couple of weeks, send him or her a private e-mail asking for clarification or further expansion of some point he or she made. Do you get an answer? If so, how would you describe the answer?

4. In a thread from either the newsgroup or the listserv, try to find an example of:

   a. Flaming

   b. An unsupported assertion

c. A misreading of someone's post

d. An especially convincing argument

e. An obviously biased poster

5. Find two different lists or newsgroups dealing with roughly the same topic. Contrast them: the tone, the willingness to either disagree or engage in verbal combat, the unwritten and unspoken assumptions behind the postings.

6. What is the difference between a search engine and a directory (a.k.a. index)?

7. What are the parts of a URL? Give an example of a URL and explain what each part means.

8. What is a query?

9. Explain in your own words how the AND operator limits a category and the OR operator expands a category.

10. Is the Boolean phrase "(coffee AND cream) OR sugar" the same as "coffee AND (cream or sugar)"? Why or why not?

11. Explain in your own words how Boolean operators and other logical operators work in a query. Give an example of a complex query, using both Boolean and other logicals, and explain how it will be read by a search engine. What kinds of information do you expect it to find?

12. Use that query in your favorite search engine. Are there any surprises?

13. Enter a simple search with minimal Boolean operators into Excite. How many documents does it find? Enter the same search into Alta-Vista. How many documents does it find? How do the two searches contrast?

14. Begin keeping a personal chart for yourself of the strengths and weaknesses of each of the major search engines. Keep adding to it as you gain more experience with Web searching.

15. Browse the Yahoo! Directory (http://www.yahoo.com/). Find a general topic you think might be worth pursuing in a research paper; follow Yahoo!'s links to narrow that topic down and to find some initial sites where potentially useful information may be stored.

The Warmups

Let's begin warming up with some practice queries and Boolean phrases.

1. Compose a Boolean phrase that describes a group of desserts that are pies and that are either apple or peach.

_____

_____

_____

iSearch: English

2. Compose a Boolean phrase that describes a group of desserts that are pies of all kinds except cherry.

_____

_____

3. Construct a query for Alta Vista that will find, in the first ten hits, when Galileo was born. Try it; refine it if necessary.

_____

_____

4. Construct a query for AltaVista that finds sites opposed to the Endangered Species Act.

_____

_____

5. Try the query from question 4. What do you find? How can you refine
your search to focus more closely on the goal?

_____

_____

_____

The Hunt (WWW)

In the early days of the Internet, there was a monthly contest called "The
Internet Hunt," in which one of the few users of the Net would pose a
problem for the other few users, and the first one to find the answer on
the Internet (and provide documentation for how she did it) won. Once
the Internet grew to hundreds of thousands and finally tens of millions of
users, the contest became unwieldy and it was discontinued. But it was a
good idea—many a budding Internet researcher cut teeth on this contest.

So for practice, here is a list of new "Internet Hunts" for you to try out
your new research skills. For each question, provide:

1. The answer
2. The URL where you found the answer
3. The process you used (most likely, the query phrase and the search
   engine used, and perhaps the intermediate links you clicked on)

All of these questions will be answerable from the World Wide Web
(or occasionally from its predecessors Gopher or FTP—all accessible via
your Web browser.) There will often be a variety of correct answers to parts
2 and 3—the Web is notorious for providing multiple paths to the same
points.

Questions

1. Where is Karl Marx buried (city, country, cemetery)?

   Answer:

   _____

   _____

   URL:

   _____

   _____

Process:

_____

_____

_____

2. What is the name of the Greek astronomer who calculated the circumference of the Earth over 1,500 years before Columbus sailed?

Answer:

_____

_____

_____

URL:

_____

_____

_____

Process:

_____

_____

_____

3. According to Grant himself, what does the middle initial "S" stand for in "Ulysses S. Grant"? (Note: it's not "Simpson.")

Answer:

_____

_____

_____

URL:

_____

_____

_____

iSearch: English

Process:

_____

_____

_____

4. How many blue whales are left on planet Earth?

Answer:

_____

_____

_____

URL:

_____

_____

_____

Process:

_____

_____

_____

5. How many hours a day does the average American child watch television?

Answer:

_____

_____

URL:

_____

_____

_____

iSearch: English

Process:

_____

_____

_____

6. What woman led the fight to clean up Love Canal in the 1970s?

Answer:

_____

_____

_____

URL:

_____

_____

_____

Process:

_____

_____

_____

7. Who coined the term "rock and roll"?

Answer:

_____

_____

_____

URL:

_____

_____

_____

iSearch: English

Process:

_____

_____

_____

8. In what year did it become illegal for employers to discriminate against people with physical disabilities?

Answer:

_____

_____

_____

URL:

_____

_____

_____

Process:

_____

_____

_____

9. Browse the Yahoo! directories (not its Web-search function) for this one: What percentage of the population of Nepal is under the age of 18?

Answer:

_____

_____

URL:

_____

_____

_____

Process:

_____

_____

_____

10. How many times did Robert Frost win the Pulitzer Prize?

Answer:

_____

_____

_____

URL:

_____

_____

_____

Process:

_____

_____

_____

For Discussion

Share the results in class with others. Did you all find the answers?

If someone couldn't find one, why? What was he or she doing wrong?

As a class, begin to formulate some helpful tips for finding Internet resources that seem to work for the whole class.

How many different sites did your class find with the same answer to any particular question?

And finally, did others in the class find different answers to the same question? (Many sites, for example, repeat without comment the incorrect information about Ulysses S. Grant's middle name being "Simpson"— would you have stopped after the first site that said that, if you hadn't been told that it was incorrect?) How do you interpret the different answers to the same question?

iSearch: English

A Closer Look at Hunting

Now try this:

Use the same relatively complex search query in three or four different search engines (or as close to the same as the particular engine's rules allow).

The Query:

_____

_____

Run the searches on the same day. What do you find?

Engine _____

Number of Hits _____

URL of First (i.e., "most relevant") hit _____

_____

Engine _____

Number of Hits _____

URL of First (i.e., "most relevant") hit _____

_____

Engine _____

Number of Hits _____

URL of First (i.e., "most relevant") hit _____

_____

Engine _____

Number of Hits _____

URL of First (i.e., "most relevant") hit _____

_____

Citation Exercise

Write the "Works Cited" entry for one of the sites above in perfect MLA format.

_____

_____

_____

_____

_____

Do the same one in perfect APA format.

_____

_____

_____

_____

For Class Discussion

There very likely are huge differences in the information found. What are they? How do you explain them?

Do any of the engines miss what appears to be an extremely relevant site that another (or most) of the engines find?

Can you draw any inferences about the relative strengths and weakness of each search engine. Is more always better? Is less always better?

Can you think of any situations where you would prefer one engine over another?

What do you wish the engines could do that they don't do?

Beyond Search Engines

Using the resources from the following page but not using any of the search engines:

1. Find the complete text of a poem or play by a British author who lived before 1700.
2. Find a Web site devoted to an author you're reading in your composition class.
3. Find the meaning of "cerumen" using an online dictionary.
4. What does the acronym SPELL stand for?
5. What's wrong with this sentence: "Every dog must have it's day"? Where did you find the answer?
6. Find the text of Maya Angelou's poem read at the 1993 inauguration of President Clinton.
7. In Aristotle's _On Interpretation_, what must he first define?
8. What's the rule in English grammar for forming the possessive of a singular noun that ends in _s_?

iSearch: English

9. The quote "We are such stuff as dreams are made of" is actually a misquote. What is the correct quote, and where is it found?

More English Activities

1. Create a small Web site based on the topic of one of your writing assignments from your composition class.
2. Find the e-mail address of a writer you've read (or read about) in your composition class. Send him or her an e-mail with a question or comment on the reading. Do you get an answer?
3. Get the e-mail addresses of a few of your classmates and submit a draft of a paper you're working on to Redline. Have them respond. How helpful are services like this?
4. When you have a question of grammar and usage in your writing, submit it to one of the OWLs. How helpful and authoritative is the answer you receive?

iSearch: English

Online Resources

Internet Sites Useful to English

AltaVista

Ask Jeeves

Britannic Internet Guide

http://www.eb.com/

From the Encyclopedia Britannica people; evaluates, rates, and limits findings.

Google Groups

http://groups.google.com

Searches Usenet newsgroups.

Excite

HotBot

Infoseek

Lycos

WebCrawler

Yahoo!

http://www.yahoo.com/

Both a full-fledged WWW search engine and the most famous directory for browsing.

Fee-Based Research Services

Dun & Bradstreet

http://www.dnb.com/

DNB is the leading provider of business-to-business credit, marketing, purchasing, and receivables management and decision-support services worldwide. Search for corporate information and buy reports.

Electric Library

http://www.elibrary.com/

Allows plain English searches of more than 150 full-text newspapers and 800 full-text magazines; free 30-day subscription.

Lexis-Nexis

http://www.lexisnexis.com

Online legal, news, and business information services.

Thomas Register of American Manufacturers

`http://www.thomasregister.com/`

This site allows users to buy and specify from manufacturers of millions of industrial products and services.

UnCover

`http://www.carl.org/`

A periodical index and document delivery (by fax) service.

General Directories

Berkeley Digital Library

`http://sunsite.berkeley.edu`

The online collection at the University of California; searchable.

Complete Reference to Usenet Newsgroups

`http://www.tile.net/tile/news/`

A searchable listing of Usenet groups.

InfoSurf: E-Journals and E-Zines

http://www.library.ucsb.edu/mags/mags.html

A categorically arranged list of magazines and journals available electronically.

LIBCAT

http://www.metronet.lib.mn.us/lc/lc1.cfm

Comprehensive guide to libraries (United States and worldwide) that have Internet presence.

Librarian's Index to the Internet

http://sunsite.berkeley.edu/InternetIndex/

This site has hundreds and hundreds of links arranged by major categories and subcategories to almost every topic of interest.

Libweb: Library Servers via WWW

http://sunsite.berkeley.edu/Libweb/

Directory of online libraries in 62 countries; searchable by location or affiliation.

LISTSERV Lists Search

http://tile.net/listserv/

A searchable listing of e-mail discussion groups (listservs).

Social Science Information Gateway

http://sosig.esrc.bris.ac.uk

A comprehensive listing of social science information sources available electronically worldwide.

Supreme Court Decisions

http://www.law.cornell.edu/supct/

A searchable database of recent Supreme Court decisions.

Voice of the Shuttle: Web Page for Humanities Research

`http://vos.ucsb.edu/index.asp`

An amazingly comprehensive directory of humanities-oriented Web pages.

Desktop References

Acronym and Abbreviation List

`http://www.ucc.ie/info/net/acronyms/`

Searchable list of acronyms; also reversible to search for acronym from a keyword.

The Acronym Finder

`http://www.mtnds.com/af/`

Type in an acronym and this site will search its collection of 75,000 to find a match.

The Alternative Dictionaries

`http://www.notam.uio.no/~hcholm/altlang/`

Dictionary of slang and expressions you most likely won't find in a normal dictionary; all entries are submitted by users.

CIA World Factbook

`http://www.odci.gov/cia/publications/factbook/`

Every hard fact about every country in the world.

Computing Dictionary

`http://wombat.doc.ic.ac.uk/`

Dictionary of computing terms; often technical.

iSearch: English

Encarta

http://www.encarta.msn.com

Microsoft's Encarta encyclopedia allows users to keyword search topics and offers other education-related features.

Encyclopedia.com from Electric Library

http://www.encyclopedia.com/

This online encyclopedia allows the user to search a term/phrase or browse by letter.

InfoPlease

http://www.infoplease.com/

Combines the contents of an encyclopedia, a dictionary, and several up-to-the minute almanacs loaded with statistics, facts, and historical records.

The King James Bible

http://etext.virginia.edu/kjv.browse.html

In addition to a searchable KJV, this site provides a side-by-side comparison of the King James and the Revised Standard.

Discovery School

http://school.discovery.com/students/index.html

The Discovery Channel's school site is a great homework helper. Users will find study tools, challenging games, and "learning adventures" to explore to find a perfect school project.

Quotations Page

http://www.tqpage.com

Search for that quotation by keyword.

Roget's Thesaurus

http://humanities.uchicago.edu/forms_unrest/ROGET.html

An online searchable version of the venerable book of synonyms.

Scholes Library Electronic Reference Desk

`http://scholes.alfred.edu/ref_desk/ref.html`

An index of "ready reference" sources.

Shakespeare Glossary

`http://eserver.org/langs/shakespeare-glossary.txt`

Alphabetically arranged text file of words from Shakespeare; not a concordance.

Writing Help

Anti-Pedantry Page: Singular "Their" in Jane Austen and Elsewhere

`http://uts.cc.utexas.edu/~churchh/austheir.html`

A compilation of famous writers who've ignored the singular "their" rule.

Bartlett's Familiar Quotations

`http://www.bartleby.com/quotations/100/`

1901 edition. Searchable.

Basic Prose Style & Mechanics

`http://www.rpi.edu/web/writingcenter/handouts.html`

This site offers various pamplets on citation styles, writing styles, and kinds of writing including cover letters, critiques, and even lab reports.

BGSU Online Writing Lab

`www.bgsu.edu/offices/acen/writerslab/handouts.html`

A site with downloadable grammar and writing tips.

iSearch: English

The Blue Book of Grammar & Punctuation

http://www.grammarbook.com/

Use this site to find answers about questions on proper English grammar and punctuation.

Capitalization

http://stipo.larc.nasa.gov/sp7084/sp7084ch4.html

According to NASA's Handbook.

Dakota State University Online Writing Lab (OWL)

http://www.departments.dsu.edu/owl/

An Online Writing Lab that provides writing help via e-mail.

DeVry Online Writing Support Center

http://www.devry-phx.edu/lrnresrc/dowsc/default.htm

Resources for integrating the Internet into your college composition classes.

The Online English Grammar

http://www.edufind.com/english/grammar/toc.cfm

Over a hundred short discussions of grammatical topics.

Elements of Style

http://www.bartleby.com/141/index.html

Will Strunk's 1918 classic.

English Grammar FAQ as posted to alt.usage.english

http://www-personal.umich.edu/~jlawler/aue/
    index.html

Answers to common grammar questions from linguist John Lawler.

Garbl's Writing Resources On Line

`http://www.garbl.com`

This site has many links to help the user write the perfect paper. These links are split into English grammar, style, usage, plain language, words, reference sources, online writing experts, word play, and books on writing.

A Glossary of Rhetorical Terms with Examples

`http://www.uky.edu/ArtsSciences/Classics/rhetoric.html`

Forty-five rhetorical terms (Alliteration to Zeugma) with links to classical text for examples.

Grammar and Style Notes

`http://andromeda.rutgers.edu/~jlynch/Writing/`

Alphabetically arranged guide to topics in grammar and style. Includes a collection of grammatical rules and explanations, comments on style, and suggestions on usage.

Glossary of Poetic Terms

`http://www.poeticbyway.com/glossary.html`

A unique guide to the study of poetry. Features phonetic pronunciation, cross references, broad range of definitions, numerous examples, hyperlinked keywords and cross references, a wealth of poetic quotations, and writers' guidelines

HyperGrammar

`http://www.uottawa.ca/academic/arts/writcent/`
   `hypergrammar/intro.html`

Hypertext grammar course/handbook from the University of Ottawa.

The "It's" vs. "Its" page

`http://www.fred.net/kathy/its.html`

The difference between the two homophones.

iSearch: English

The King's English

http://www.bartleby.com/116/

Full text of H. W. Fowler's 1908 classic on English, Victorian-style.

Main Writing Guide

http://www.english.uiuc.edu/cws/wworkshop/index.htm

Three complete online handbooks for writing.

Nebraska Center for Writers

http://mockingbird.creighton.edu/NCW/

Online resource for writers of poetry, fiction, and creative non-fiction.

On-line English Grammar

http://www.edunet.com/english/grammar/

Especially suited for non-native speakers of English; includes some sound files.

Online Writery

http://web.missouri.edu/~writery/

"The conversation zone for writers"; tutors and writers meet online and discuss writing.

Paradigm: Online Writing Assistant

http://www.powa.org/

Almost a complete writing textbook online.

PEN Home

http://www.pen.org/

The home page of PEN, the professional association of writers and editors.

Poets and Writers Inc. Home Page

`http://www.pw.org/`

Support for professional writers and those who would be professional writers.

Politics and the English Language

`gopher://dept.english.upenn.edu/00/Courses/Lynch3/`
`   orwell`

Full text of George Orwell's plea for clarity in writing and thinking.

Punctuation

`http://stipo.larc.nasa.gov/sp7084/sp7084ch3.html`

Punctuation according to NASA.

Purdue On-Line Writing Lab

`http://owl.english.purdue.edu/`

An extensive source of online help for writers, including professional help to specific questions by e-mail.

Rensselaer Writing Center Handouts

`http://www.rpi.edu/web/writingcenter/handouts.html`

A collection of handouts on writing topics from "abstracts" to "writing with gender-fair language."

Researchpaper.com

`http://www.researchpaper.com/`

An impressive compendium of research-paper help, including live chat rooms.

iSearch: English

The Ruth H. Hooker Research Library and Technical Information Center

http://infoweb2.nrl.navy.mil/index.cfm

A collection of sites for all writing needs. Users will find links to dictionaries, Bartlett's quotations, encyclopedias, and more.

Tips and Resources for Writers

http://www.tipsforwriters.com/

Materials for professional writers that are appropriate for beginners as well.

Undergraduate Writing Center

http://uwc.fac.utexas.edu

Services restricted to University of Texas students and staff; links to resources for writers.

Gayle Morris Sweetland Writing Center OWL at the University of Michigan

http://www.lsa.umich.edu/swc/

Receive advice about your writing via e-mail and browse links to other writing resources.

The University of Victoria's Hypertext Writer's Guide

http://web.uvic.ca/wguide/

Hypertext guides to writing and literature.

The Word Detective

http://www.word-detective.com/

Online version of the newspaper column answering questions about words.

Writing Centers Online

http://iwca.syr.edu

A directory of writing centers nationwide who have online presences.

Writing Help from the College of Wooster

`http://www.wooster.edu/writingctr/help.html`

The College of Wooster's Writing Center has posted information on rules of grammar, comma usage, and other helpful hints. Documentation help is also offered at this site.

Writing Papers of Literary Analysis: Some Advice for Student Writers

`http://unix.cc.wmich.edu/cooneys/tchg/lit/adv/`
`   lit.papers.html`

From Western Michigan University.

Writing References from Ohio State

`http://osunlabs.newark.ohio-state.edu/`
`   writing-lab/ref.htm`

The Ohio State Writing Lab presents useful tools for any type of composition, in any type of discipline. These references include *Webster's Dictionary*, *Oxford English Dictionary*, *Rogêt's Thesaurus*, and 130 grammar handouts compiled by Purdue University.

Writing for the Internet

Barebones Guide to HTML

`http://www.werbach.com/barebones/`

This site offers detailed information on HTML by listing every official HTML tag in common usage, plus Netscape and Microsoft extensions.

CNET's Builder.com

`http://builder.com/`

This site offers detailed information and tips for all aspects of Web site development.

iSearch: English

Dictionary of PC Hardware and Data Communications Terms

http://www.ora.com/reference/dictionary/

This comprehensive dictionary provides complete descriptions of complex terms in two of the most volatile and interesting areas of computer development: personal computers and networks.

Everything E-Mail

http://everythingemail.net/

Everything you ever wanted to know about e-mail.

HTML Validator

http://www.htmlhelp.com/tools/validator/

Provides a service that allows users to input URL(s) to make sure that they are HTML compatible.

HTML Writers Guild

http://www.hwg.org/

Assists in developing and enhancing the capabilities of web authors while contributing to the web standards and guidelines. Find information about standards, techniques, and ethics as applied to Web authoring.

Student Web Pages

http://www2.haverford.edu/acc/webdev/html.html

Student-oriented guide from Haverford College

MOO Help

http://www.du.org/dumoo/moohelps.htm

Basic MOO techniques and commands from Diversity University.

Criteria for Evaluation of Internet Information Resources

`http://www.vuw.ac.nz/~agsmith/evaln/index.htm`

From an online Internet resources course from Victoria University, New Zealand.

NCSA Beginner's Guide to HTML

`http://www.ncsa.uiuc.edu/General/Internet/WWW/`
   `HTMLPrimer.html`

For those times when you have to tinker under the hood of your Web pages.

User Guide to Netiquette

`http://www.learnthenet.com/english/html/09netiqt.htm`

How to behave, electronically speaking.

Web Writers

`http://www.whidbey.net/servsup/useful.html`

This site has many links to help the user create a Web site. There are links to pages that help the process of setting up Web pages on WhidbeyNET, Web writing references, Web creation, how to register a site, JAVA, and backgrounds and graphics for a Web site.

WWWScribe: Web Resources for Writers

`http://www.wwwscribe.com/`

Writing for the WWW, along with using the Internet as a research and communication tool.

Evaluating Information on the Internet

Checklist for Evaluating Web Sites

http://www2.canisius.edu/canhp/Searching_the_Internet/
    Evaluating_Internet_Resources/

Tips from the Canisius University Library.

Critically Analyzing Information

http://www.library.cornell.edu/okuref/research/
    skill26.htm

Not specifically devoted to Internet information sources.

Evaluating Internet Information

http://www.library.jhu.edu/elp/useit/evaluate/

Specific guidance from Johns Hopkins University.

Evaluating Internet Research Sources

http://www.virtualsalt.com/evalu8it.htm

A comprehensive essay, not just a checklist.

Evaluating Quality on the Net

http://www.hopetillman.com/findqual.html

An excellent and continually evolving paper from Hope Tillman, Babson
College.

Internet Tutorial: Evaluating Internet Resources

http://www.cst.edu/Library/EvalIntRes.html

A short document from the Claremont School of Technology.

World Wide Web Site Evaluation for Information Professionals

`http://www.unc.edu/cit/guides/irg-49.html`

This site offers the user many links to evaluating Web site resources. Periodical evaluation is also available here.

Specialized Web Sites

Abortion and Reproductive Rights Internet Resources

`http://www.caral.org/abortion.html`

An extensive set of links to information both pro-choice and pro-life.

Alex: A Catalog of Electronic Texts on the Internet

`http://www.infomotions.com/alex/`

A listing of full-length texts available on the Internet.

African Americana

`http://www.lib.lsu.edu/hum/african.html`

A moderately extensive directory of Web sites (and more) dealing with the African American experience.

The American Civil War Home Page

`http://sunsite.utk.edu/civil-war/warweb.html`

U.S. Civil War information is categorized by general resources, documented records, specific battles, civil war reenactors, the secession crisis and before, histories, Civil War round tables, and more. There are hundreds of links at this site.

American Poetry Hyper-Bibliography

`http://www.hti.umich.edu/a/amverse/`

A Web-based guide to American poetry prior to 1920, searchable on author or title.

American Studies Web

http://www.georgetown.edu/crossroads/asw/

A good jumping off point for studies in Americana.

AstroWeb: Astronomy/Astrophysics on the Internet

http://www.cv.nrao.edu/fits/www/astronomy.html

An extensive directory of links and a searchable database of topics in astronomy.

Best of the Christian Web

http://www.botcw.com/

This site has collected Christian sites in all categories. A good starting point for anyone looking for Chistian information and media.

Essays in History—University of Virginia

http://etext.lib.virginia.edu/journals/EH/

Full text of the journal *Essays in History* issues since 1990.

FAQ: How to Find People's E-mail Addresses

http://www.faqs.org/faqs/finding-addresses/

A guide to the often frustrating process of finding an e-mail address.

Fedworld Information Network

http://www.fedworld.gov/

The searchable gateway to the huge information resources of the federal government.

Feminist Activist Resources on the Net

http://www.igc.org/women/feminist.html

A compilation of useful links to feminist resources.

Film—Media Resources

```
http://www.miracosta.cc.ca.us/home/gfloren/
    FilmRes.htm
```

This site provides comprehensive information and links to film and media. Categories include specific movie Web sites, screenplays, award ceremonies, movie history, genres, special effects, discussion groups and chat rooms, and more.

GPO Access Databases

```
http://www.access.gpo.gov/su_docs/multidb.html
```

Another guide to government publications, online and print versions (with instructions for ordering print documents).

The Human-Languages Page

```
http://www.ilovelanguages.com
```

A huge compendium of links to resources in language.

Internet Movie Database

```
http://us.imdb.com/
```

A keyword-searchable database of everything you ever wanted to know about movies.

Journals

```
http://english-server.hss.cmu.edu/journals/
```

Alphabetical listing (with links) to hundreds of journals, both print-based and electronic, that have a Web presence; from Carnegie-Mellon's Humanities Server.

Library of Congress

```
http://lcweb.loc.gov/
```

The jumping off point for the Library's online resources; not the whole Library itself, however.

Liszt

http://www.liszt.com

A searchable and browsable guide to listservs (e-mail discussion lists).

Media History Project

http://www.mediahistory.umn.edu

A gateway to information on communications and media studies; searchable.

National Center for Education Statistics

http://www.nces.ed.gov/

Department of Education site containing statistics on education in the United States.

National Center for Health Statistics

http://www.cdc.gov/nchswww/default.htm

The repository of the Center for Disease Control's data.

NASA Spacelink

http://spacelink.msfc.nasa.gov/

NASA's fulfillment of its obligation to disseminate all the information it gathers through space exploration.

The National Center on Addiction and Substance Abuse

http://www.casacolumbia.org/

The Web page of the think tank devoted to providing resources on understanding the abuse of illegal substances.

National Organization for Women

http://www.now.org/calendar/html

A collection of on-site information and links to other Web sites for women's issues.

Nijenrode Business Webserver

`http://library.nijenrode.nl/INT/index.html`

Searchable guide to online business resources, focused on the needs of students, faculty, and researchers.

On-Line Literary Resources

`http://andromeda.rutgers.edu/~jlynch/Lit/`

A searchable categorized directory of extensive academic sources of information in English and American literature.

Postmodern Culture

`http://jefferson.village.virginia.edu/pmc/`
`    contents.all.html`

Complete collection of the online journal of post-modernism.

Resources for Diversity

`http://www.nova.edu/`

A compilation of links to resources in issues of diversity.

Rhetoric and Composition

`http://eserver.org/rhetoric/`

An extensive guide to rhetoric, from the ancients to modern composition theory.

Suicide Information and Education Center (SIEC)

`http://www.siec.ca/`

Onsite resources, information, and links to more sites on issues of suicide prevention.

Thomas

`http://Thomas.loc.gov/`

A searchable database of all bills before the most recent sessions of the House of Representatives.

United States Census Bureau Home Page

http://www.census.gov

A gold mine of statistics about the U.S. population.

U.S. Department of Education

http://www.ed.gov/

This site provides educational information in the form of programs, news, services, educational publications, and grant information for educators, researchers, and parents.

U.S. Senate

http://www.senate.gov/

A guide to business of the U.S. Senate.

University of Virginia Electronic Text Library

http://etext.lib.virginia.edu/

Provides access to the University of Virginia's extensive collection of digitized texts and images.

Voice of the Shuttle: Web Page for Humanities Research

http://vos.ucsb.edu/

An amazingly comprehensive directory of humanities-oriented Web pages.

Welfare and Families

http://epn.org/ideacentral/welfare/index.html

The Electronic Policy Network's electronic journal, archives, and links.

White House

http://www.whitehouse.gov/WH/Welcome.html

The starting point for Executive Branch information.

World Intellectual Property Organization (WIPO)

`http://www.wipo.org/`

A guide to resources on copyrights and patents in the electronic age.

World Wide Arts Resources

`http://wwar.world-arts-resources.com/`

A searchable gateway to the arts online, plus a directory of Web sites, chats and bulletin boards.

Current Events

CNN

`http://www.cnn.com/`

Multimedia, up-to-the minute online news source; not adequately archived for searches.

Electronic Newsstand

`http://www.enews.com/`

An extensive listing of thousands of magazines.

Forbes

`http://www.forbes.com/`

Online version of *Forbes Magazine*; searchable archives.

Fox News

`http://www.foxnews.com/`

News, business, health, sports, and technology.

The New York Times on the Web

`http://www.nytimes.com/`

The New York Times on the Web. Requires registration, but free.

The New York Times on the Web: Books

`http://www.nytimes.com/books/`

Web-based book section of the *Times*.

Newsstand

`http://www.newsdirectory.com`

Links to over 4,200 Web sites of print publications—newspapers, magazines, computer publications. Searchable by publication name.

San Francisco Chronicle

`http://www.sfgate.com/chronicle/`

Online version; searchable.

Time Magazine

`http://www.time.com`

An online version of *Time Magazine*; search feature searches *Time* and many others; also provide access to bulletin boards and chats.

TotalNEWS

`http://totalnews.com/`

According to itself, "Information is the oxygen of the modern age. TotalNEWS is a directory of news sites designed to increase your access to information."

USA TODAY

`http://www.usatoday.com/`

Online version of the national newspaper.

Washington Post

http://www.washingtonpost.com/

Online version of the *Washington Post*; searchable for past week.

Bibliographic Citation Guides

American Psychological Association (APA) Guide to Style

http://www.wpunj.edu/library/apa.htm

Online version of the *APA Guide*; abridged.

Bibliographic Styles Handbook: APA

http://www.english.uiuc.edu/cws/wworkshop/index.htm

A hypertext index to the APA publication style, from the University of Illinois at Urbana-Champaign.

Columbia Online Style

http://www.columbia.edu/cup/cgos/basic.html

The Alliance for Computers and Writing-endorsed guide to documenting online sources.

MLA Style

http://www.mla.org/

The official site of MLA and its most current guide to publication style.

Modern Language Association (MLA) Guide to Style

http://www.wpunj.edu/library/mla.htm

Online version of the *MLA Guide;* abridged.

iSearch: English

Finding E-mail Addresses

Bigfoot

`http://www.bigfoot.com`

Supposedly the Internet's largest collection of e-mail addresses.

People Search

`http://people.yahoo.com`

Yahoo! searches for people's e-mail addresses. The user types in the person's first and last name and then clicks enter.

Four11

`http://www.411locate.com/`

An extensive searchable e-mail address directory, plus "yellow pages," a phone book, government, and celebrity addresses.

Internet Address Finder

`http://www.iaf.net/`

Claims to be the fastest e-mail search engine, with nearly six million addresses in its database.

Phonebook

`http://www.phonebook.com/`

Searches Yahoo!, Usenet, and its own e-mail address database.

Switchboard

`http://www.switchboard.com/`

One of the most popular "people-finders" on the Internet; good for addresses and phone numbers, thin on e-mail addresses.

Usenet Addresses Database

`http://usenet-addresses.mit.edu/`

A list of the e-mail addresses of posters to Usenet (actually a huge number, when you think about it).

WhoWhere

`http://www.whowhere.com/`

One of the first, and still one of the most used, people finders: e-mail addresses, phone numbers, home pages, business and government Web and e-mail addresses, 800 numbers, yellow pages, and more.

World E-mail Directory

`http://www.worldemail.com/`

Spreads itself thin, but your best chance at finding a non-U.S. address.

Other Online Resources

Companion Websites

`http://www.abinteractive.com/gallery`

Our Companion Websites use the Internet to provide you with various opportunities for further study and exploration. The Companion Website offers study content and activities related to the text, as well as an interactive, online study guide. Quizzes containing multiple choice, true/false, and essay questions can be graded instantly, and forwarded to your instructor for recording—all online. For a complete list of titles with a Companion Website, visit www.abinteractive.com/gallery.

Flash Review Series for Introduction to Grammar

`http://www.flashreview.com`

This is the Companion Website to the Flash Review for Introduction to Grammar, a new kind of study guide that features interactive quizzes, career advice, sample tests, and study aides. You can find a copy of the study guide at your local bookseller.

iSearch: English

ContentSelect

What is ContentSelect?

http://www.ablongman.com/contentselect

The ContentSelect Research Database gives you instant access to thousands of academic journals and periodicals *any* time from *any* computer with an Internet connection. With new features like **Start Writing!** and **Citing Sources** to help you find and cite valid sources, starting the research process has never been easier!

New features help you write your research papers:

- **Start Writing!** includes detailed information on the process of writing a research paper, from finding a topic, to gathering data, using the library, using online sources, and more.

- **Internet Research** and **Resource Links** feature links to many of the best sites on the Web, providing tips and best practices to help you quickly find resources on the Web.

- **Citing Sources** show you how and when to cite sources and includes examples of various citation styles, from the best-selling book on research papers.

The ContentSelect research database engine has also been improved to make it even easier to use—now you can:

- Search across multiple discipline-specific journal collections
- Search popular culture periodicals
- Refine searches, after an initial search has returned results.
- Print and e-mail journal articles, with or without citations

Now the ContentSelect Research Database is the easiest way to start a research paper!

How to Use ContentSelect

To begin exploring the great resources available in the ContentSelect Research Database Web site:

Step 1:   Go to:

http://www.ablongman.com/contentselect

Step 2:   The resources on the home page will help you start the research and writing process and cite your sources. For invaluable research help,
- Click **Citing Sources** to see how to cite materials with these citation styles: MLA, APA, CMS, and CBE.
- Click **Start Writing!** for step-by-step instructions to help you with the process of writing a research paper.
- Click **Resource Links** and **Internet Research** to link to many of the best sites on the Web with tips to help you efficiently use the Web for research.

Step 3:   Register! To start using the ContentSelect Research Database, you will need to register using the access code and instructions located on the inside front cover of this guide. You only need to register once—after you register, you can return to ContentSelect at any time, and log in using your personal login name and password.

Step 4:   Log in! Type in your login name and password in the spaces provided to access ContentSelect. Then click through the pages to enter the research database, and see the list of disciplines. You can search for articles within a single discipline, or select as many disciplines as you want! To see the list of journals included in any database, just click the "**complete title list**" link located next to each discipline—check back often, as this list will grow throughout the year!

Step 5:   To begin your search, simply select your discipline(s), and **click "Enter"** to begin your search. For tips and detailed search instructions, please visit the "ContentSelect Search Tips" section included in this guide.

For more help, and search tips, click the Online Help button on the right side of your screen.

Go to **www.ablongman.com/contentselect** now, to discover the easiest way to start a research paper!

ContentSelect Search Tips

Searching for articles in ContentSelect is easy! Here are some tips to help you find articles for your research paper.

Tip 1: **Select a discipline.** When you first enter the ContentSelect Research Database, you will see a list of disciplines. To search within a single discipline, click the name of the discipline. To search in more than one discipline, click the box next to each discipline and click the **ENTER** button.

Basic Search

The following tips will help you with a Basic Search.

Tip 2: **Basic Search.** After you select your discipline(s), you will go to the Basic Search Window. Basic Search lets you search for articles using a variety of methods. You can select from: Standard Search, Match All Words, Match Any Words, or Match Exact Phrase. For more information on these options, click the *Search Tips* link at any time!

Tip 3: **Using AND, OR, and NOT** to help you search. In Standard Search, you can use AND, OR, and NOT to create a very broad or very narrow search:

- **AND** searches for articles containing all of the words. For example, typing **education AND technology** will search for articles that contain **both** education AND technology.
- **OR** searches for articles that contain at least one of the terms. For example, searching for **education OR technology** will find articles that contain either education OR technology.
- **NOT** excludes words so that the articles will not include the word that follows NOT. For example, searching for **education NOT technology** will find articles that contain the term education but NOT the term technology.

Tip 4: **Using Match All Words.** When you select the "Match All Words" option, you do not need to use the word AND—you will automatically search for articles that only contain all of the words. The order of the search words entered in does not matter. For example, typing **education technology** will search for articles that contain **both** education AND technology.

Tip 5: **Using Match Any Words.** After selecting the "Match Any Words" option, type words, a phrase, or a sentence in the window. ContentSelect will search for articles that contain any of the terms you typed (but will not search for words such as **in** and **the**). For example, type **rising medical costs in the United States** to find articles that contain *rising, medical, costs, United,* or *States.* To limit your search to find articles that contain exact terms, use *quotation marks*—for example, typing "United States" will only search for articles containing "United States."

Tip 6: **Using Match Exact Phrase**. Select this option to find articles containing an exact phrase. ContentSelect will search for articles that include all the words you entered, exactly as you entered them. For example, type **rising medical costs in the United States** to find articles that contain the exact phrase "rising medical costs in the United States."

Guided Search

The following tips will help you with a Guided Search.

Tip 7: To switch to a Guided Search, click the **Guided Search** tab on the navigation bar, just under the EBSCO Host logo. The *Guided Search Window* helps you focus your search using multiple text boxes, Boolean operators (AND, OR, and NOT), and various search options.

To create a search:

- Type the words you want to search for in the Find field.

- Select a field from the drop-down list. For example: AU-Author will search for an author. For more information on fields, click *Search Tips*.

- Enter additional search terms in the text boxes (optional), and select *and, or, not* to connect multiple search terms (see Tip 3 for information on *and, or,* and *not*).

- Click **Search**.

Expert Search

The following tips will help you with an Expert Search.

Tip 8: To switch to an Expert Search, click the **Expert Search** tab on the navigation bar, just under the EBSCO Host logo. The *Expert Search Window* uses your keywords and search history to search for articles. Please note, searches run from the Basic or Guided Search Windows are not saved to the History File used by the Expert Search Window—only Expert Searches are saved in the history.

Tip 9: Expert Searches use **Limiters** and **Field Codes** to help you search for articles. For more information on Limiters and Field Codes, click *Search Tips*.

Explore all the search options available in ContentSelect! For more information and tips, click the Online Help button, located on the right side of every page.

iSearch: English

Glossary

Your Own Private Glossary

The Glossary in this book contains reference terms you'll find useful as you get started on the Internet. After a while, however, you'll find yourself running across abbreviations, acronyms, and buzzwords whose definitions will make more sense to you once you're no longer a novice (or "newbie"). That's the time to build a glossary of your own. For now, the ZDnet Webopædia gives you a place to start.

alias   A simple e-mail address that can be used in place of a more complex one.

AVI   Audio Video Interleave. A video compression standard developed for use with Microsoft Windows. Video clips on the World Wide Web are usually available in both AVI and QuickTime formats.

bandwidth   Internet parlance for capacity to carry or transfer information such as e-mail and Web pages.

BBS   Bulletin Board System. A dial-up computer service that allows users to post messages and download files. Some BBSs are connected to and provide access to the Internet, but many are self-contained.

browser   The computer program that lets you view the contents of Web sites.

client   A program that runs on your personal computer and supplies you with Internet services, such as getting your mail.

cyberspace   The whole universe of information that is available from computer networks. The term was coined by science fiction writer William Gibson in his novel *Neuromancer*, published in 1984.

DNS   See **domain name server**.

domain   A group of computers administered as a single unit, typically belonging to a single organization such as a university or corporation.

domain name   A name that identifies one or more computers belonging to a single domain. For example, "apple.com."

domain name server   A computer that converts domain names into the numeric addresses used on the Internet.

download   Copying a file from another computer to your computer over the Internet.

e-mail   Electronic mail.

emoticon   A guide to the writer's feelings, represented by typed characters, such as the Smiley :-). Helps readers understand the emotions underlying a written message.

FAQ   Frequently Asked Questions.

flame   A rude or derogatory message directed as a personal attack against an individual or group.

flame war   An exchange of flames (see above).

FTP   File Transfer Protocol. A method of moving files from one computer to another over the Internet.

home page   A page on the World Wide Web that acts as a starting point for information about a person or organization.

hypertext   Text that contains embedded *links* to other pages of text. Hypertext enables the reader to navigate between pages of related information by following links in the text.

LAN: Local Area Network. A computer network that is located in a concentrated area, such as offices within a building.

link   A reference to a location on the Web that is embedded in the text of the Web page. Links are usually highlighted with a different color or underlined to make them easily visible.

list server   Strictly speaking, a computer program that administers electronic mailing lists, but also used to denote such lists or discussion groups, as in "the writer's list server."

lurker   A passive reader of an Internet *newsgroup*. A lurker reads messages, but does not participate in the discussion by posting or responding to messages.

mailing list   A subject-specific automated e-mail system. Users subscribe and receive e-mail from other users about the subject of the list.

modem   A device for connecting two computers over a telephone line.

newbie   A new user of the Internet.

newsgroup   A discussion forum in which all participants can read all messages and public replies between the participants.

pages   All the text, graphics, pictures, and so forth, denoted by a single URL beginning with the identifier "http://".

plug-in   A third-party software program that will lend a Web browser (Netscape, Internet Explorer, etc.) additional features.

quoted   Text in an e-mail message or newsgroup posting that has been set off by the use of vertical bars or > characters in the left-hand margin.

search engine   A computer program that will locate Web sites or files based on specified criteria.

secure   A Web page whose contents are encrypted when sending or receiving information.

server   A computer program that moves information on request, such as a Web server that sends pages to your browser.

Smiley   See **emoticon**.

snail mail   Mail sent the old fashioned way: Write a letter, put it in an envelope, stick on a stamp, and drop it in the mailbox.

spam   Spam is to the Internet as unsolicited junk mail is to the postal system.

URL   Uniform Resource Locator. The notation for specifying addresses on the World Wide Web (e.g., http://www.ablongman.com or ftp://ftp.ablongman.com).

Usenet   The section of the Internet devoted to newsgroups.

Web browser   A program used to navigate and access information on the World Wide Web. Web browsers convert html coding into a display of pictures, sound, and words.

Web site   A collection of World Wide Web pages, usually consisting of a home page and several other linked pages.

iSearch: English

Notes: